THE 6 PRINCIPLES FOR EXEMPLARY TEACHING OF ENGLISH LEARNERS®

ACADEMIC AND OTHER SPECIFIC PURPOSES

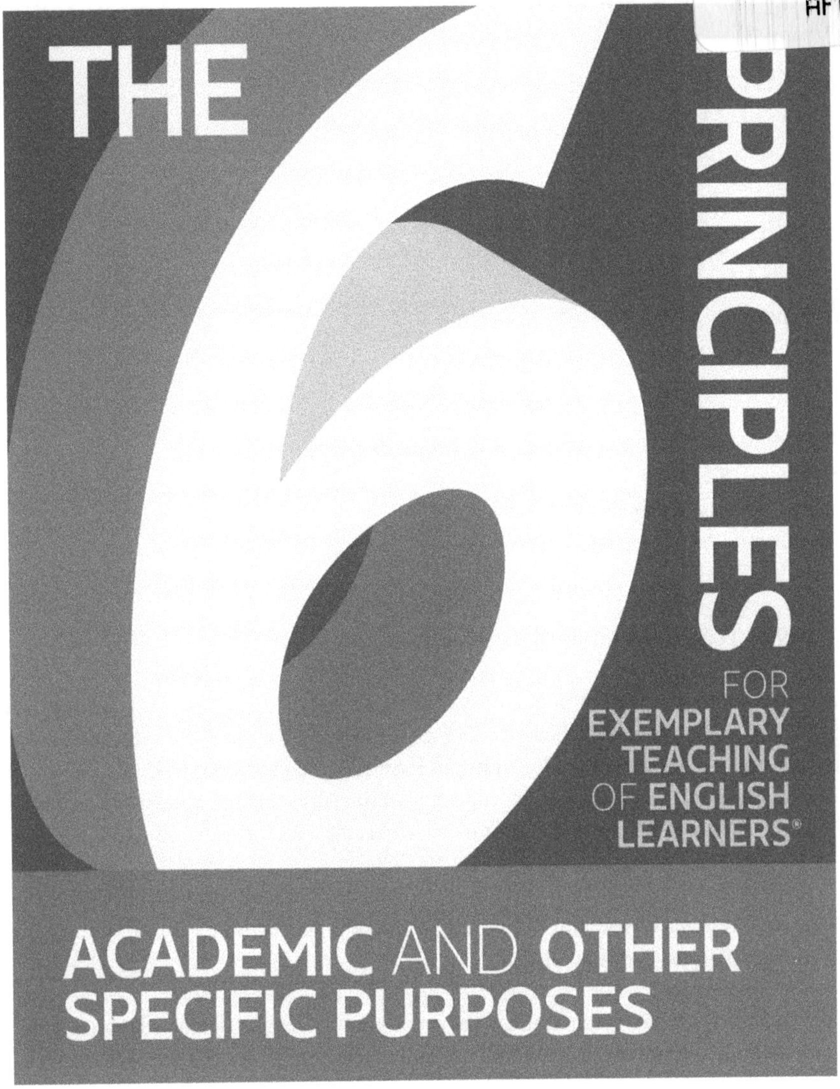

Sherry Blok
Robyn Brinks Lockwood
Evan Frendo

Deborah J. Short, *Series Editor*

FOREWORD **BY ANDY CURTIS**

This book has a companion website. Go to www.the6principles.org/eap-esp for additional resources.

www.tesol.org/bookstore

TESOL International Association
1925 Ballenger Avenue
Alexandria, VA 22314 USA
www.tesol.org

Director of Publishing and Product Development: Myrna Jacobs
Copy Editor: Deborah Kennedy
Cover and Interior Design: Citrine Sky Design
Layout: Capitol Communications, LLC
Printing: Gasch Printing, LLC

Copyright © 2020 by TESOL International Association

All rights reserved. Copying or further publication of the contents of this work is not permitted without permission of TESOL International Association, except for limited "fair use" for educational, scholarly, and similar purposes as authorized by U.S. Copyright Law, in which case appropriate notice of the source of the work should be given. Permission to reproduce material from this book must be obtained from www.copyright.com, or contact Copyright Clearance Center, Inc., 222 Rosewood Drive, Danvers, MA 01923, 978-750-8400

The 6 Principles for Exemplary Teaching of English Learners® and The 6 Principles® are registered trademarks of TESOL International Association, Inc.

Every effort has been made to copyright holders for permission to reprint borrowed material. We regret any oversights that may have occurred and will rectify them in future printings of this work.

Recommended citation:
Blok, S., Lockwood, R. B., & Frendo, E. (2020). *The 6 principles for exemplary teaching of English learners: Academic and Other Specific Purposes*. Alexandria, VA: TESOL International Association.

ISBN 978-1-945351-686
ISBN 978-1-945351-693
Library of Congress Control Number 2018963975

PURCHASE ORDERS AND
BULK PURCHASES
Discounts are available for
tax-exempt purchase orders and
bulk purchases. Please contact
publications@tesol.org for
more information.

First edition, 2020
1 2 3 4 5 6 7 8 9 10

CONTENTS

Foreword by Andy Curtis v
Preface vii
Acknowledgments xi

CHAPTER 1

Teaching English for Specific Purposes with The 6 Principles 1
    English for Specific Purposes 2
    Types of ESP Courses 3
    Key Factors in Teaching ESP. 4
    Profiles of ESP Learners 7
    The 6 Principles for Exemplary Teaching of English Learners 9
    A Look Back and a Look Ahead 10

CHAPTER 2

What Teachers Should Know about English Language Development to Plan Instruction . . . 11
    Why Learn English in an ESP Setting? 12
    What Adults Bring to Learning in ESP Settings 13
    How ESP Learners Learn Best 14
    Developing Language Proficiency for Academic and Other Specific Purposes 16
    Characteristics of ESP 17
    Conditions for Second Language Learning 24
    English Language Proficiency Levels 28
    Standards for Second Language Learning 30
    The Role of Language in Identity 31
    A Look Back and a Look Ahead 32

CHAPTER 3

Teaching with The 6 Principles for Academic and Other Specific Purposes 35
    The 6 Principles for Exemplary Teaching of English Learners and
        Recommended Practices 36
    Principle 1. Know Your Learners 37
    Principle 2. Create Conditions for Language Learning 41
    Principle 3. Design High-Quality Lessons for Language Development 47
    Principle 4. Adapt Lesson Delivery as Needed 61

  Principle 5. Monitor and Assess Learner Language Development 65
  Principle 6. Engage and Collaborate within a Community of Practice. 71
  A Look Back and a Look Ahead 73

CHAPTER 4

Establishing a Culture of Shared Responsibility 75
  Institutional Leaders 76
  ESP Program Administrators 81
  Academic Faculty 85
  Guidance and Learning Counselors. 90
  A Look Back and a Look Ahead 92

CHAPTER 5

The 6 Principles in Different Program Contexts 93
  Passing the TOEFL iBT Test 93
  An Academic Writing Course at a German University 98
  A Large MBA Business English Class in India 102
  Training Sales Engineers to Negotiate in English 106
  Preparing Indonesian Healthcare Workers for Overseas Employment. 110
  A Look Back and Final Observations 114

Appendix: Self-Assessment: The 6 Principles Checklist for Teachers. 117

Glossary 121

References 127

FOREWORD

I am grateful for the opportunity to write the foreword to this important book, the third in *The 6 Principles for Exemplary Teaching of English Learners®* series. This book focuses on English for academic and other specific purposes (ESP) and was written by Sherry Blok, Robyn Brinks Lockwood, and Evan Frendo, who bring an international perspective to the project. Although the six principles on which this series is based are universal and apply to all English language teaching and learning situations, TESOL International Association is acutely aware that one size does *not* fit all. As a reflection of that understanding, the first book addresses the principles in K–12 settings (TESOL, 2018) and the second book applies these principles in adult education and workforce development contexts (Hellman, Harris, & Wilbur, 2019). This book is designed to enable all ESP teachers to make use of these principles in their classrooms with their learners.

As far as we know, all human civilizations throughout history have told stories (Curtis, 2020), and this book begins with a brief narrative about teacher 'Kendra' and her learners, who are "a group of four managers from the same company that she has been teaching every week for the last two months." This chapter structure, beginning with a vignette from the classroom, is significant because it shows how the day-to-day experiences of English language teachers and learners form the basis of this series and of this book. We begin in the classroom because that is where real life happens for us. I continue to read other publications that distinguish between 'the classroom' and 'real life' with dismay, but for everyone involved in *The 6 Principles* series and in this book, the English language classroom is as real as it gets.

TESOL professionals are some of the busiest teachers in the education field, holding down multiple teaching positions in different places at the same time. As a result, we have limited time for and patience with 'grand theorizing' (Curtis, 2017). That is one of the reasons why this book will be warmly welcomed by many ESP teachers, as it offers a great deal of practical advice, presented clearly and concisely, which is an achievement in itself considering how much the different fields of ESP have grown over the years. Examples of how this book is anchored in the daily, classroom (virtual and traditional) realities of English language teaching and learning are the profiles of adult learners presented in Chapter 2 and the five robust cases of implementation in different types of ESP programs in Chapter 5.

In Chapter 2, the authors acknowledge that, although "[t]he 6 Principles are not new concepts . . . they build on the findings of several decades of research on second language acquisition and English language teaching." The authors go on to explain that these six principles "are consistent with the recommendations found in several syntheses of research on second language education" and that "they represent an assets-based approach, which views English learners' first languages and cultures as resources to draw on." For those of us who have spent much of our lives in classrooms as language teachers and learners, such an approach may sound like common sense. However, as Rhonda Scharf pointed out in the title of her 2009 book, *Common Sense is NOT Common Practice*.

The breadth and depth of The 6 Principles are seen in Chapter 3, where the main principles are divided into nearly 20 sub-principles. For example, Principle 3 is: 'Design High-Quality Lessons for Language Development.' Great advice, but how? To answer that question, the authors have split Principle 3 into seven practices, such as 3a: 'Teachers determine language and content objectives for their classes,' and 3g: 'Teachers promote students' self-regulated learning.' Most importantly, in order to ensure that the research-based understandings on which The 6 Principles are based can be realized in ESP classrooms, each of the practices has multiple examples of ways in which teachers apply a particular principle effectively in their classrooms.

The final two chapters, 'Establishing a Culture of Shared Responsibility' and 'The 6 Principles in Different Program Contexts' are, like the previous chapters, filled with research-informed practical advice and concrete examples that connect theory and practice in ways that are mutually edifying. Chapter 4 will help teachers work with others, such as administrators, faculty, and curriculum developers, serving as not only as resources to fellow educators, but advocates for the learners at a time when international student enrolments are at their highest in English-speaking countries. Chapter 5, as mentioned above, showcases classes and programs that implement the principles and give readers a view of a typical classroom lesson in five very diverse contexts.

During my three years in the presidential line of TESOL International Association (2014–2017), I had the pleasure, the privilege, and the honor of sitting in ESP classrooms all over the world. Looking back on those observations, I cannot think of a single class I saw that would not have benefited in some way from the ideas in this book.

Andy Curtis
Anaheim University, Anaheim, California, USA
50th President (2015–2016) TESOL International Association

PREFACE

English for Specific Purposes (ESP) plays a critical role internationally as adult learners acquire English for study, work, and life. ESP is "an approach to language teaching that targets the current and/or future academic or occupational needs of learners, focuses on the language, skills, discourse and genres to address these needs, and assists learners in meeting these needs through general and/or discipline-specific teaching and methodologies" (Anthony, 2015). The term ESP thus refers to the skills, knowledge, and competencies that are required to understand and function within a specific discourse community.

The field of ESP has come into increasing prominence as globalization has motivated adult learners to advance their English language skills. Currently, one in four people in the world is reported to learn and use English for personal, academic, or professional purposes. English is the fastest growing language in human history and has become the lingua franca in the science, technology, and business sectors (Neeley, 2012).

As knowledge of English has become the gateway to education and employment in many contexts, different types of ESP programs have arisen to address adults' associated learning needs. In academic settings, English for academic purposes (EAP) programs employ different models, including intensive English programs (IEPs), content and language integrated learning (CLIL), and programs that prepare learners for "the spread of English as a medium of instruction (EMI) within communities where English is not the primary language of communication" (EMI Oxford Research Network, 2019; Kırkgöz & Dikilitaş, 2018). EAP courses and programs focus on teaching the language of the academic disciplines as well as the skills and strategies needed for success in academic work in English; these skills and strategies may, by cultural practices, vary from one country to the next. In workplace and professional contexts, ESP programs may focus on English for occupational purposes (EOP, also referred to as workplace language training), where adults are seeking to develop the English language skills they need for their jobs, or English for professional purposes (EPP), where adults are pursuing greater proficiency in the language of their fields of expertise, such as business, law, government, medicine, and other professions (Friedenberg et al., 2014).

The 6 Principles

English language teaching is a dynamic field, which is highly impacted by technological advancements. This calls for continuous learning and support for instructors[1] in all English as a second language (ESL) and English as a foreign language (EFL) contexts, including those in ESP.

TESOL International Association advances the expertise of English language teachers and brings together professional learning, research, standards, and advocacy. TESOL strives to be the trusted global authority for knowledge and expertise in English language teaching. Its mission is to advance the quality of English language teaching around the world.

---

[1] The term instructors may be used as synonymous with the term teachers.

On TESOL's 50th anniversary in 2016, the association launched a strategic initiative to define the shared principles for exemplary teaching of English learners in the many contexts where English is taught. The diversity of learners and the varied learning environments have made this charge particularly challenging. A writing team and many expert reviewers from within and outside of the association engaged with a passion to identify The 6 Principles and describe the practices that characterize them. The goal was to reflect the state of the art in language teaching practice and research in The 6 Principles while delivering these findings in a user-friendly way so teachers could apply them.

The 6 Principles are at the root of exemplary teaching. These statements cultivate innovation and growth and provide a basis for informed decision-making and intentional planning with learners. All English language teachers can relate to them:

1. Know your learners.
2. Create conditions for language learning.
3. Design high-quality lessons for language development.
4. Adapt lesson delivery as needed.
5. Monitor and assess student language development.
6. Engage and collaborate within a community of practice.

The 6 Principles anchor each teacher to the foundational practices of exemplary educators. The 6 Principles framework will guide the design of effective lessons that support learners and move their learning forward. This framework allows TESOL International to convey the most important elements of expertise in the field to anyone with a desire to understand and improve the education of English learners.

The first volume in *The 6 Principles for Exemplary Teaching of English Learners* series addresses exemplary teaching for English learners in K–12 schools in the United States (TESOL, 2018). The second volume focuses on teaching English in adult education and workforce development programs; the applications feature inner-circle English-speaking countries where English is the majority language (Hellman, Harris, & Wilbur, 2019).

The current volume shows the same principles in action when teaching adult learners for academic and other specific purposes in a broad international context. It is written for instructors of those adult learners who are studying English specifically to advance their professional, occupational, or academic goals. Some of those learners have learning goals that are immediate and very specific; some may have been learning English throughout their primary, secondary, and college years, and well into their careers. Each learner's experience with English will vary; implementing The 6 Principles enables instructors to meet them where they are and help them reach their goals.

Audience

The intended audience for this book includes

- Teachers and trainers working in a range of contexts, such as
    — Higher education institutions, including intensive English programs (IEPs) and community colleges
    — Work-related professional courses and programs, such as English for engineers, or English for aviation, or English for legal professionals
    — Private language institutes (PLIs)
    — Adult education programs
    — Workplace language training programs

- Teachers working in support of academic faculty
- Teachers of preparation courses for standardized language tests such as IELTS, TOEFL, and CAEL
- TESOL educators training tomorrow's teachers
- Consultants providing advice to organizations, including education institutions, corporations, and government ministries

The secondary audience is

- Administrators of ESP courses and programs
- Language mentors for specific purposes
- Administrative staff on ESP-related courses and programs
- Institutional leaders in academic programs and private language centers
- Materials writers for ESP courses and programs
- Curriculum developers
- Directors of Studies in language schools
- Counselors and learning skills specialists
- Training managers and human resource managers

Overview

This volume presents the principles and practices of exemplary teaching in five chapters:

Chapter 1: Teaching English for Specific Purposes with The 6 Principles, introduces ESP, outlines various types of programs and courses, and discusses key factors that need to be considered. It also provides sample learner profiles and an introduction to using The 6 Principles in teaching.

Chapter 2: What Teachers Should Know about English Language Development to Plan Instruction, summarizes the main factors related to learning a new language for ESP learners and covers topics such as tapping into preexisting resources that learners bring to the classroom and understanding the features of academic and professional English. The chapter will help language instructors make informed decisions for lesson planning.

Chapter 3: Teaching with The 6 Principles for Academic and Other Specific Purposes, defines and illustrates each principle and supplies several high-leverage practices that add depth and clarity to what each principle means. The chapter elaborates on the principles because instructors must consider each as they plan and deliver instruction. The chapter offers many ideas that can be implemented in a variety of ESP settings.

Chapter 4: Establishing a Culture of Shared Responsibility, suggests ways in which institutional leaders in academic programs and private language centers, program administrators, academic faculty, and training managers can apply The 6 Principles in their spheres beyond the classroom. By working together, they can ensure that English language learners receive quality programs and services designed to support their language development needs and foster educational success in a positive and enriching environment.

Chapter 5: The 6 Principles in Different Program Contexts, shows how to facilitate exemplary teaching in different teaching environments by applying The 6 Principles framework. The chapter features English instructors and their adult learners in five different programs around the world. All of the instructors deliver high quality lessons consistently but for varied purposes. The chapter points out where and how The 6 Principles are in action in these contexts, to demonstrate what they look and sound like in a variety of courses as a guide for instructors implementing them in their own teaching.

Moving Forward

The 6 Principles framework is an important strategy for achieving TESOL's mission of advancing the quality of English language teaching around the world. The writing team for the current volume accepted the charge to build on the existing framework and adapt it for teaching adult learners with specific professional, occupational, and academic language goals. The team was able to achieve this by altering some practices slightly where necessary and adding several new teaching practices. This book is a springboard to the vast branch of language teaching known as ESP; it cannot cover each situation in which ESP teaching takes place, but it includes a variety of examples and vignettes across the five chapters to illustrate different scenarios which instructors can relate to.

This volume is consistent with the others in The 6 Principles series, and with it we join the movement that the original work started. We are excited to share our experience in this book and highlight how you as an ESP instructor can implement The 6 Principles in your classrooms, courses, and programs. We hope that you will join us and make your mark, not only by implementing these principles with your classes but also by joining TESOL International Association as a member and bringing The 6 Principles to your community of practice. Please join us in advancing the field.

Sherry Blok
Robyn Brinks Lockwood
Evan Frendo

ACKNOWLEDGMENTS

Dedicated and passionate English language educators across diverse global contexts impact the lives of their learners by adopting best practices in teaching and training. They contribute to a wealth of knowledge to develop our understanding of second language acquisition and the teaching practices that best facilitate the development of our learners. We thank them for their contributions to this project by sharing their experiences through their work and by telling their own stories.

We express our gratitude to the TESOL International Board of Directors and central office staff for their ongoing support of The 6 Principles initiative. We would like to acknowledge Myrna Jacobs, Director of Publishing and Product Development, and Christopher Powers, Executive Director. Particular thanks goes to the original 6 Principles writing team, Helene Becker, Nancy Cloud, Andrea Hellman, Linda New Levine, and Deborah Short. Without their groundbreaking work, this volume would not be possible. Warmest thanks to Deborah Short, The 6 Principles series editor, for her vision and guidance throughout the process. Thank you to Georgios Kormpas for providing early assistance in the development of some chapters and to Andrea Hellman, whose work we built on for Chapter 2. We also appreciate Deborah Kennedy for her developmental and copy editing work, and offer our sincerest gratitude to Andy Curtis for writing the Foreword.

A special note of thanks goes out to all of the reviewers who contributed their time to provide their professional insights and detailed feedback to strengthen the book. Our reviewers are international researchers and practitioners of ESP, some of whom are TESOL members and others from TESOL affiliates. All are invested in the development of their learners and in adopting the most effective teaching and learning practices.

Shahid Abrar-ul-Hassan	Jena Lynch	Constance Rylance
Scott Douglas	Andrea Lypka	Sarah Sahr
Michael Joseph Ennis	Gilda Martinez-Alba	H. Douglas Sewell
Marvin D. Hoffland	Cheiron McMahill	Gabrielle Smith
Mark Krzanowski	Margarita Mitevska	Kay Westerfield
Li-Fen Lin	Cathy Raymond	Ke Xu

DEDICATION

To our learners, who inspire us and give meaning to our work—
and to our colleagues, who do the same.

1 TEACHING ESP WITH THE 6 PRINCIPLES

Kendra works in a private language school in Buenos Aires, Argentina. One of her classes is a group of four managers from the same company that she has been teaching every week for the last two months. She has assessed their language skills, shadowed them at work, and learned about their jobs. The course outline was agreed with the participants at the beginning of the course, and covers a variety of business communication skills. This week the focus is on presentation skills. She starts the class by asking the learners to think about recent meetings with clients and suppliers, and share the types of presentations they have seen or given. She then asks them to list what made the presentations particularly good or bad. The list is wide ranging, from business issues such as content and accuracy of information, to presentation skills such as rapport with audience and use of visual aids, to specific language issues such as pronunciation, spelling, and the ability to handle questions.

Kendra explains that these are all key issues which the class will examine over the next few sessions, and emphasizes that everyone's contribution will be critical as they have far more experience in their own context than she does. The aim is for everyone to have a chance to do at least two presentations on topics related to their workplaces (ideally a presentation they must give as part of their jobs), and then receive constructive feedback from the group. The criteria for success will be based on the list the class has just produced. She adds that each presentation with teacher and learner feedback can be recorded and sent to the individual concerned if that person is comfortable with this process.

She then shows the class three short videos linked to the textbook on presentations, which focus on language aspects of presentations, namely introductions, summarizing and concluding, and dealing with questions. After a brief discussion she gives out a worksheet for practicing some of the key phrases they have just heard, and which they might like to use in their own presentations. She splits the class into pairs and instructs each pair to select and practice appropriate phrases for use with their own content. The worksheet then becomes a personalized resource which can be used the next time they have to prepare a presentation, or for extra practice for outside the class.

She ends the class by asking the learners to consider what they saw on the videos and reflect further on the criteria for successful presentations. The class agrees that it would be useful to add two more items to the list: successful presentations have a clear structure, with the introduction and conclusion being particularly important, and successful presentations use signposting language to guide the audience. The learners agree that they will email Kendra the topics of their presentations before the next class.

Kendra makes notes about what happened during the class in her own personal diary. She also discusses the class with a colleague over a cup of coffee, which helps her think more carefully about what she has achieved and what she should do next time.

English for Specific Purposes

The aim of this book is to share TESOL's vision for exemplary teaching in ESP (English for Specific Purposes), and to show how useful The 6 Principles for Exemplary Teaching of English Learners are in such contexts. The principles discussed in this book provide a solid framework for teachers like Kendra to use in their day-to-day work, enabling them not only to make informed decisions about what they are doing, but also to reflect critically on their practice.

What is unique about ESP courses? Perhaps a good place to start is to suggest that, unlike learners in many "general" English courses, ESP learners have a specific purpose in mind when they enroll in an ESP course. They may need to improve their English so that they can take a higher education course where English is the medium of instruction (EMI). This means that they will be focusing on EAP (English for Academic Purposes). Or they may want to practice the specific language of their profession or occupation in order to increase their employability, meet the requirements of their workplace (English for Occupational Purposes, or EOP), or become better able to participate in professional activities on the international level (English for Professional Purposes, or EPP). Whatever the reason, the teacher's key role will be to understand each learner's needs and goals and help all learners develop their proficiency in order to narrow the gap between where they currently are and where they need and want to be.

There are two important issues here. First, unlike "general" English teaching contexts, where the teacher is probably familiar with the target discourse, ESP teachers may find that they themselves are not experts in that discourse, and so learning about the characteristics of the language they are teaching becomes part of the job. This is not only about language, but also about understanding the ways the target community of practice operates (Lave & Wenger, 1991; Wenger, 1998). Here the concept of community of practice is particularly useful for ESP teachers because it helps to explain how groups of people who have a common domain of interest not only interact with each other and share experiences and resources, but also learn from each other and develop their own ways of doing things. Chapter 3 will demonstrate in detail the pivotal nature of this concept within The 6 Principles framework, which emphasizes the importance of teachers engaging and collaborating within a community of practice. But the point here is that for anyone working in ESP, gathering and analyzing evidence, rather than relying on intuition, is critical. Indeed, one way to think about ESP might be to say it can involve the teaching of language or communication patterns that even speakers with advanced proficiency may not know. So ESP practitioners may need to

- Use corpus tools to look at the lexico-grammatical features of the target discourse
- Interview supervisors and other stakeholders to understand the tasks types and the linguistic and cultural expectations that characterize the target context
- Interview subject specialists in order to develop appropriate role-plays and simulations
- Select and adapt authentic texts for their classes
- Observe members of the community of practice in action
- Provide explicit instruction, practice and feedback on the types of tasks learners will be expected to deal with in their target contexts

Second, criteria for measuring success will depend very much on the learners' context. There is a big difference between the criteria set for international English tests, for example, which typically have considerable research supporting descriptions of what it means to be competent, and criteria in an occupational or professional context, where the uniqueness of the situation might require teachers to determine what it means to be competent through observation and interaction with various stakeholders. As we shall see, The 6 Principles provide a very useful framework to deal with these sorts of issues.

Types of ESP Courses

ESP is an overarching term that can be divided into different areas, as noted in the Preface. EAP, which is a major focus of this book due to its growing importance in universities around the world, focuses on developing language proficiency and study skills for post-secondary studies (Hyland & Shaw, 2016). EAP course types range from general courses, which typically attend to the language proficiency, analytical skills, and intercultural competences needed across academic disciplines, to more specific courses that focus on the language of a specific discipline or subject area. This range is much more complex than it sounds. Research shows that different disciplines use language in quite different ways and that developing appropriate intercultural communicative competence can be central to successful EAP instruction, so adopting a general approach may not be the most efficient way of doing things (Douglas & Rosvold, 2018; Hyland, 2012). For instance, compare a typical journal article in literature to one in engineering or mathematics: the differences are not only with terminology and phraseology, but also with how findings are presented, discussed, and analyzed. In brief, disciplines see the world through different lenses.

Nonetheless, there are plenty of language-related skills which are pertinent in any academic discipline, from listening skills (useful in lectures and discussions) to skimming and scanning written texts for information. Some EAP classes are aimed at university admission, with many learners needing to pass tests such as IELTS, TOEFL, or the Pearson Test of English–Academic. These types of tests all focus on generic language and skills rather than subject-specific ones. Within a university context, a general approach does not require teachers to become subject specialists; rather, the subject content can be integrated by subject specialists working with the language specialist as required. The issue is tricky, however; there is much debate around the world on how best to teach academic English (Hyland & Shaw, 2016). One solution adopted by many institutions is to provide general classes for first-year students, and more specific classes for those at later stages of their studies.

EPP can include business English, legal English, English for banking and finance, and English for medical research, to name a few, while EOP can be aviation English, English for the hospitality industry, maritime English, English for medical technicians, and so on. Many of these can also be subdivided, so aviation English might partition into English for cabin crews and English for pilots and air traffic control, and English for banking and finance might split into English for corporate finance and English for international banking. The divisions might not only have to do with specialized terminology or phraseology, but also with the way the language is used. Both EPP and EOP focus on language for specific work contexts; the differences between the two have to do with genre, register, vocabulary, and task types. Written EOP course materials primarily include task-focused documents such as instructions, forms, charts, and short reports, and the oral communication needs of EOP learners often include ability to interact with customers and peers using high-frequency vocabulary with some job-specific technical terms. In EPP, written materials may include journal articles, research reports, briefs, and analyses. Oral communication tasks may include presentations and meeting management as well as basic interpersonal interaction, and both oral and written language functions may involve negotiation and persuasion (Lesiak-Bielawska, 2015).

Many ESP courses, depending as always on the needs of the learners, will also address other transferable skills, such as intercultural communication, relationship building, teamwork, critical thinking, and leadership talk. Likewise, subject matter knowledge will almost always influence an ESP course–it is hard to read a text on engineering, for example, without knowing anything about engineering. Here the teacher will often rely on the learners' own experience and knowledge.

ESP courses are very often viewed along a continuum. At one end of the continuum are what are sometimes described as narrow-angle courses, focusing on learners with very similar language needs for a particular context. At the other end are wide-angle courses, focusing on learners who have identified a shared focus, but perhaps have less similar needs than those found on the narrow angle course (Basturkmen, 2006). So managers from different companies attending a class which focuses on general business communication skills, such as giving presentations, handling negotiations, or writing emails, would be attending a "wider-angle" class than a group of managers from one company who are learning those skills within the context of their own company's salesforce needs. Likewise, managers from one department in that company would be able to focus much more on their specific needs, so they might only look only at certain types of presentations or negotiations or emails rather than at skills more relevant to other departments. In ESP, the term "specific" is relative, rather than absolute, but provides a useful way to describe what a course is about.

It is important to remember that the distinctions between EAP, EOP, and EPP are not always clear cut. Consider a university course in legal English; much of the language covered will be just as useful when the learners have left the university and are following their profession. However, it is also worth remembering that some of the academic language needed at university might never be used in professional life. For example, most automotive engineers will never have to write an academic article once their university training is over, and the communication skills they do need (such as for supervising technicians and negotiating contracts) may never have been part of their academic English course.

Key Factors in Teaching ESP

Needs Analysis. The concern with specificity means that needs analysis is a fundamental feature of all ESP courses. Of course, all English teaching should be aimed at meeting learner needs, but what makes ESP different is not "the *existence* of a need as such, but rather an *awareness* of the need" (Hutchinson & Waters, 1987). Brown (2016) describes needs analysis as "the systematic collection and analysis of all information necessary for defining and validating a defensible curriculum." Dudley Evans and St John (1998) say it is what is needed to establish "the *what* and *how* of a course." Huhta and colleagues (2013) see needs analysis as taking "account not just of the individual, but also of how that individual interacts in the contexts and situations of his or her field of action."

Keep the following points in mind when conducting a needs analysis:

- First, the information ESP teachers collect and analyze is used to find the gap between what learners already know and what they need to know in order to function effectively in their target context. It may include information about the learners, language use in that context, and information about a wider social context.
- Second, a needs analysis typically involves many people, from the teacher and the learners in the classroom, to a potentially wide range of other stakeholders who have some interest in what is happening or who can provide useful information which helps to describe the gap mentioned above. All these people will influence what happens in a course.

- Third, a needs analysis is ongoing, not something that happens before a course begins. A teacher will always have to adapt to new information and new perspectives as the course progresses.
- Finally, for any needs analysis, it is never possible to collect and analyze *all* the information that is available, so a needs analysis is very much a compromise between an ideal world, where we have as much information as we need, and the real world, where we are dealing with what is realistically possible. (Friedenberg et al., 2014)

Vocabulary. An important part of any ESP course design is vocabulary, with a particular focus on the specialized use of words in a specific context. Researchers have produced countless word lists of technical vocabulary in different fields of expertise, ranging from medicine to engineering to general academic vocabulary. Such lists can be useful when designing ESP courses, but it is always important to remember that every context is different, and the vocabulary taught in an ESP course will always depend on the specific needs of the learners. One of the key challenges is working with vocabulary that has a specific meaning in a particular context. For this reason, many teachers and materials developers in ESP contexts use an applied corpus linguistics approach that draws on directly relevant authentic materials. This allows them to identify the frequency with which specialized terms are used; more importantly, it allows them to move beyond thinking about vocabulary as individual words to thinking about vocabulary in terms of word combinations, words related to a concept, or bundles of words (Chung & Nation, 2003; Coxhead, 2013; Hyland, 2008).

Genre. Within ESP, John Swales has been particularly influential in developing a focus on genre, seeing it as "a class of communicative events" (Swales, 1990). In this sense a genre is much more than a type of text—it is about understanding what language use is conventional and acceptable in a particular community. As Flowerdew (2011) notes, "Someone participating in a genre who does not have a command of these specific patterns and the limits to their possible variability is quickly recognized as either incompetent or an outsider." Bhatia (2008) argues that anyone analyzing genre in an ESP context also needs to look at the relevant professional and disciplinary practices and cultures.

Genre was in evidence at the beginning of the chapter, in the example of Kendra and her teaching of presentation skills. Flowerdew's observation is particularly pertinent here: Kendra's aim is to make sure her learners are not seen as incompetent or outsiders. Presentations can be seen as an example of one type of genre, but it would also be correct to think more discretely—sales presentations, academic talks, technical briefings, and so on. Genre is merely a label for certain communicative events, and the label's definition depends entirely on the context. An EAP course might focus on essay writing, but could teach different sub-genres, such as argument essays or problem-solution essays. A business English course might look at types of small talk, from office gossip to storytelling, but a course preparing German business people to work in the United States might approach small talk differently from one preparing them to work in China.

Methodologies. Teachers can use different approaches and methodologies to teach language in an ESP context, and the decisions they make often depend on the type of ESP they are teaching. For example,

- in a class for MBA students, a case study approach might be particularly appropriate (see the vignette in Chapter 5);
- in an EAP class focusing on argumentative essay writing, a scaffolded approach might be the best way forward, where the learners might be required to deconstruct a text, analyze key ideas, focus on linking language, and then produce a short text themselves;

- in a one-to-one workplace context, the teacher might be shadowing the learner as they go about their daily work, giving advice and feedback as necessary; or
- in a business English class, role plays reflecting the types of situations the learners will meet might be more useful, so the focus might be on giving presentations, taking part in meetings, and so on.

This last approach is an example of task-based language learning, where the aim is to focus on meaning rather than form, and where success is measured by whether the learners achieve their goal in the task, rather than on accuracy of language production. So, for example, in a course teaching English for the workplace, a task may be to role-play a conversation about a problem with a supplier, with success being measured on whether the nature of the problem is fully understood and communicated by the learners, rather than on whether the grammar used was accurate. ESP learners can easily identify with and see the relevance of using such activities, and such an approach can be highly motivating.

Content-based instruction (CBI) and project-based instruction (PBI) are related in many ways to task-based learning. In CBI, subject matter and language learning are integrated. Learners focus on the subject matter, and language learning is approached holistically, rather than being broken down into discrete items to be analyzed and learned. PBI typically involves the learners working in collaboration and using a wide range of skills and knowledge in order to solve a problem or challenge or complete a project. Again the focus is on meaning rather than form. In these contexts, it is common to see the teacher take on different roles, such as facilitator or coordinator, in order to be most effective.

Global Englishes. English is used all over the world, which means that there is no one "standard" or "correct" English, but rather many Englishes. Researchers have looked at this phenomenon in different ways.

- A "World Englishes" perspective basically sees English in terms of varieties, such as American English, Singapore English, and so on.
- Kachru's three-circle model, which sees English in terms of inner circle countries (e.g., United States, United Kingdom), outer circle countries (e.g., India, Tanzania, Philippines), and expanding circle countries (e.g., China, Japan, Korea) has been particularly influential.
- An English as a lingua franca (ELF) perspective sees English more as context specific, with the participants adapting and using their language to suit the setting, using communication strategies like code switching, accommodation, and creative use of language to facilitate understanding and negotiate meaning (Jenkins, 2007; Seidlhofer, 2011). This perspective on English makes error correction particularly challenging, because deciding what is and is not correct depends on the context. This is not only about spelling or grammar, where even major varieties like American or British English may disagree. "Non-American" pronunciation, for example, does not require correction if it does not interfere with communication; indeed it may be seen as an important factor in a person's identity. Having an Indian English accent may be perfectly acceptable in India, but may be less acceptable if the learner works in a call center speaking to clients in North America. These sorts of issues are very relevant to teachers of ESP, who need to be aware of what is and is not acceptable in their learners' target discourse communities.

Profiles of ESP Learners

To illustrate some of the differences between the types of courses that can be offered in ESP, here are six profiles of ESP learners.

Johanna is a German computer programmer. She has recently finished her degree in computer science and is just starting her first full-time job. Because much of the computer science literature is in English, she is very comfortable with most English texts in her chosen profession, and she can also converse in most social situations. She is joining a team that is writing code for a turbine factory in China, and her specific role will be to liaise with other members of the team (mostly Indians) as well as representatives of the client (mostly Chinese) and ensure that change requests are handled efficiently. She has just had her first conference call, however, and realizes she has a major problem—although she can understand the discussions about the coding, she has discovered that her vocabulary related to turbines is very limited, and she is not sure she has understood the clients' feedback. Her boss understands the situation completely, and gives her permission to do a crash course in English.

Guan Lee is very excited. He has just graduated from high school in Singapore, and has been accepted in an undergraduate program at an American university to study physics. Because the course will be delivered in English, his acceptance is conditional. He must pass a pre-sessional EAP course run by the university's intensive English program (IEP) at the university in the summer months. This will be a big challenge, as he feels he is not good at English. After all, he wants to be a physicist, not a language expert. However, the IEP course will help Guan Lee acclimate to living in a new environment, as it offers many bridging activities to university life. He will learn about campus services, clubs, and events while he is improving his language and study skills in order to enter undergraduate study in the fall.

Yu Yan is in Vancouver, Canada, hoping to earn her PhD in Pharmaceutical Sciences in three years and find work as a research assistant. So far, she has done very well, and although the course is in English, she has been able to understand lectures and discussions without too much difficulty. However, her written work has been more challenging, and she is worried that she will struggle when the time comes to write her research dissertation, which she will have to complete before she graduates. Her university offers a course in English for medical purposes, and she now feels that it might be a good idea to enroll. However, having had a quick look at the course content, she is not sure if the course will offer what she is looking for. She decides to find a language instructor and ask for advice.

Yulya has finished her PhD in Mathematics (in Ukrainian, her native tongue) and her academic career is progressing well. She is a popular lecturer at her university, and she has already published three articles in Ukrainian peer-reviewed journals. So far, she has resisted learning English—she has never really needed it and has preferred to focus on Russian as her main second language. However, she has just had an interview with the dean, and two things she heard made her realize that she will have to change her strategy. The first was not surprising—the dean mentioned that if Yulya wanted to progress in her career, she would have to start presenting at international conferences and writing articles for English language journals. The second was that the university had decided that starting next year certain courses would be offered in English, the aim being to attract international students and keep the university solvent. Her courses were on the list, and she now has three months to prepare.

Abdou has worked as a sales engineer in a company in Cameroon for nearly his whole adult life. The company specializes in the repair of turbines, and Abdou's job was to sell the company's services to various clients across Central Africa. He is looking forward to his retirement and a well-earned pension in five years' time. He has already identified a small plot of land near his house and has nearly saved up enough money to buy it. He is really looking forward to spending hours on the plot and knows exactly which crops he will grow. However, today he has had news which concerns him greatly. The factory he works for has just been bought by an American competitor, and staff cuts are almost certain. He knows that his experience as a sales engineer will stand him in good stead, but he also knows that his lack of English will not work in his favor. His new supervisor will be American, and he has heard that all communication will be in English from now on. Abdou has never spoken a word of English in his life, and now his whole future may depend on it. He has no chance of getting another job as well paid as this one. The good news is that the new company is organizing English language courses. He has already signed up.

Fuying is a middle manager in a small company in Taiwan. She is good at her job, knows everybody, and is considered an asset to her boss and the company. She is very pleased that the company is so profitable, although she realizes that her company is facing fierce competition in the marketplace and that the comfortable situation will not last forever. She is already thinking about her future and her options. In order to be more employable, she will need to improve her English skills, and maybe even pass a test. Getting a high score on a TOEIC test seems her best bet. She has checked the websites of local language schools, and she has also looked at some online courses. Many TOEIC preparation courses are available on the market, and she knows that one benefit will be that she may meet others in a similar position as herself. She is looking forward to starting, but cannot decide which course to choose. She decides to take a trial class at a school and make her decision later.

As is evident, the types of courses these learners will need vary, even though they can all be described as English for a specific purpose. Guan Lee's course is clearly EAP, but much more general than the specific courses that Yulya and Yu Yan require. Note that EAP courses are not only aimed at university students—they may be targeted at faculty too. Both Johanna's and Abdou's needs involve the learning of "turbine" English, but their backgrounds and contexts will mean that the courses are completely different. Johanna knows nothing about turbines, but her English is already quite good. Abdou, on the other hand, is well versed in turbine technology (at least in his own specific area), but has no English at all. Fuying is looking for a general business English class, and will have no problem finding one, but there is no guarantee that the course will enable her to meet other middle managers, or that the language she learns will be useful in the future.

The 6 Principles for Exemplary Teaching of English Learners

The 6 Principles presented and discussed in this book are based on well-established research and experience in all aspects of teaching and learning. Together they present a framework which can be used in any language teaching context. Figure 1.1 below provides a brief explanation of each principle, with later chapters offering much more detailed discussions of how each principle can be used in the different types of ESP classrooms.

FIGURE 1.1 The 6 Principles

The 6 Principles for Exemplary Teaching of English Learners

Exemplary teaching of English learners rests on the following 6 Principles:

1. **Know your learners.** Teachers learn basic information about their learners' academic or professional goals, languages, cultures, and educational backgrounds to engage them in the classroom and prepare and deliver lessons more effectively.

2. **Create conditions for language learning.** Teachers create a classroom culture that will ensure that learners feel comfortable in the class. They make decisions regarding the physical environment, the materials, and the social integration of learners to promote language learning.

3. **Design high-quality lessons for language development.** Teachers plan lessons that are meaningful for learners and promote language learning, and help them develop learning strategies and critical thinking skills. These lessons evolve from the learning objectives.

4. **Adapt lesson delivery as needed.** Teachers continually assess as they teach—observing and reflecting on learners' responses to determine whether the learners are reaching the learning objectives. If learners struggle or are not challenged enough, teachers consider the possible reasons and adjust their lessons.

5. **Monitor and assess learner language development.** Language learners learn at different rates, so teachers regularly monitor and assess their language development in order to advance their learning efficiently. Teachers also gather data to measure learners' language growth.

6. **Engage and collaborate within a community of practice.** Teachers collaborate with others in the profession to provide the best support for their learners with respect to programming, instruction, and advocacy. They also continue their own professional learning.

A Look Back and a Look Ahead

This chapter started with a short vignette about Kendra. Take a moment to reread the vignette, and think about how Kendra applied the six principles to her course. Now read this summary:

1. Kendra has certainly spent time getting to know her learners, and within an ESP context she understands this includes developing a good understanding of their needs and goals.
2. By recognising her learners' expertise, and encouraging them to contribute to the course content, Kendra has created an atmosphere which is appropriate to an adult learning context.
3. Her lessons are clearly related to the needs of her learners, and she has broken down the language content into manageable chunks which the learners can relate to.
4. Kendra is prepared to adapt as necessary, and indeed changes her plans after receiving feedback from her learners.
5. Her decision to use personalized worksheets is an excellent way of monitoring her learners' language development, as is her decision to allow the learners to choose their own topics for the next class. This will make her feedback very relevant to each individual.
6. Briefly discussing the class afterward with a colleague allows Kendra to reflect on the lesson and collect peer feedback, and contributes to her own professional development.

This chapter has looked at what makes ESP different from other types of teaching contexts and suggested that the teacher's role in planning lessons requires much more of a focus on using evidence rather than intuition and on working with experts (including the learners) to fill gaps in knowledge or experience. The chapter has discussed different ways of thinking about ESP, considered the range of courses, and outlined some common approaches. It has also presented several learner profiles and shown how critical it is to understand where learners are coming from and what their purposes for learning English are. Even when the subject matter is similar, the specific needs of the learners make each course unique. Finally, the chapter has discussed some of the challenges and some of the decisions which need to be made, and argued that The 6 Principles framework is ideally suited to teaching these types of classes.

ESP teachers need to understand that these contexts affect the language development of learners, the dynamic nature of classrooms, and the way teachers communicate because adult learners have different reasons for acquiring English. One aspect of making choices related to ESP teaching methods and techniques is knowing how learners learn and what inhibits or facilitates their achievement of their academic or professional/occupational goals.

Chapter 2 builds on the content in Chapter 1 by looking at the main concepts of second language development specifically in ESP contexts. It covers topics such as tapping into preexisting resources that learners bring to the classroom, features of academic and professional English, and both essential and beneficial conditions for language acquisition. The chapter will help all ESP teachers make informed decisions for lesson planning, so they knowledgeably apply The 6 Principles with the learners' needs and interests in mind, propelling the learners and the teacher to success.

Additional resources for this book are available at www.the6principles.org/eap-esp.

2 WHAT TEACHERS SHOULD KNOW ABOUT ENGLISH LANGUAGE DEVELOPMENT TO PLAN INSTRUCTION

I live and work in Quebec City, a historic Canadian city, set in the province of Quebec, Canada. I am francophone and until recently only had to speak English when vacationing with my family in the USA. A recent merger with an American company has changed our company culture. I need to communicate in English with my head office in Los Angeles and clients across the States. It's challenging because despite the fact I'm university educated and have over 10 years of work experience in my field, I don't have the same reflexes in English as I do in French. Americans talk so fast and I am not sure they always understand me. I feel stressed defending my designs, pitching ideas and negotiating contracts in English. . . . I don't have a lot of time to take intensive English language training, so I need a course that is really tailored to my needs.

—Julie Gaudette, engineer

As a young boy in Vietnam I always dreamt of studying in the USA. My aunt and her family live in Baltimore, Maryland and would visit us during summer vacations. I was always amazed that my cousins could speak English and Vietnamese equally well. We would sit around the table during family dinners repeating words and phrases in English (with no idea what we were saying) and everyone would break out in laughter. Twelve years later, I'm now living with them in Baltimore, studying English in an IEP program so I can get a degree in mathematics at the University of Maryland.

—Duc Pham, learner

The 6 Principles are not new concepts. Rather, they build on the findings of several decades of research on second language acquisition and English language teaching. They are consistent with the recommendations found in several syntheses of research on second language education (August & Shanahan, 2006; Baker et al., 2014; National Academies of Sciences, Engineering, and Medicine [NASEM], 2017). More importantly, they represent an assets-based approach, which views English learners' first languages and cultures, as well as their professional knowledge and experience, as resources to draw on and make a valuable part of the classroom for the benefit of all learners.

Before delving into The 6 Principles and their implementation in Chapter 3, a brief discussion of the main concepts of second language development will be useful. Everyone has experienced learning a home language, although not all have learned a second or third language. Chapter 2 explores what it takes to learn a second language and what a vital role language plays in academic classrooms and professional workplaces.[1]

Multiple times every day instructors make decisions about how to convey information to learners and how to determine whether they understand the material and are making progress in their classes. Similarly, employers need to persuade, advise, inform, or generally convey

---

[1] Adapted from: TESOL International Association (TESOL). (2018). *The 6 principles for exemplary teaching of English learners: Grades K–12*. Alexandria, VA: Author. and Hellman, A. B., Harris. K., & Wilbur, A. (2019). *The 6 principles for exemplary teaching of English learners: Adult education and workforce development*. Alexandria, VA: TESOL International Association.

information to employees in workplace settings. Yet most college professors, employers, and colleagues are not language teachers. Language teachers and learners need to be aware that these others are not responsible for teaching English. They typically need only to present their content expertise.

All people, though, rely on language as a tool—a tool other teachers and trainers use to develop learners' content knowledge in academic or workplace settings or an employee's or colleague's knowledge about work-related tasks. Instructors explain, lead discussions, assign projects or tasks, and expect learners to complete those tasks. Each of these teaching tasks entails as much knowledge of language as knowledge of the content. Therefore, every teacher who relies on language as an instructional tool should consider their learners' need to develop the language skills that will support success in the classroom. This chapter encourages every teacher to recognize this fact, take ownership of this role, and design lessons with language learning in mind.

Knowing how the language acquisition process works and recognizing the characteristics of adult learners can help teachers with their instructional decisions, both in their planning of a lesson and in their delivery of it. If a learner makes an error in English, for example, an instructor's response should be based on whether the error is normal for a given proficiency level or indicates something that has been learned incorrectly or not at all. Effective teachers of English learners are not only conscious of their role as language teachers, but are also willing and intentional about it. They have reasonable expectations for learners because they are aware of the time, effort, and practice that it takes to learn a new language.

This chapter provides foundational knowledge for language instruction. First, it describes the assets that adult English learners possess and some characteristics of their learning styles. This material draws on the research on adult learners in general, but makes specific reference to adult learners in English for academic purposes (EAP), English for professional purposes (EPP), and English for occupational purposes (EOP) instruction. Next, the chapter looks at how academic and other specialized language can develop. Instructors need to know what their learners have to do in English before analyzing their current English proficiency levels, in order to design appropriate instruction and have reasonable expectations for what learners can do and what they need to reach the next level.

The chapter then examines essential and beneficial conditions for language learning and additional factors that may help or hinder progress. When instructors know which of these they have some control over, they can boost language learning. For example, when teachers know that language develops through use and interaction, they can plan lessons that encourage learners to use language actively and to negotiate meaning with their peers or colleagues. The chapter then discusses the basics of the English language proficiency levels that instructors in different programs use to guide placement and instructional planning and provides information on several sets of English proficiency standards that are used around the world.

Why Learn English in an ESP Setting?

Adult learners pursue educational opportunities for reasons that are integral to their everyday lives and personal and professional goals. They do not come to the learning process waiting to be filled with subject knowledge per se. They come from vastly different cultures and countries and a broad range of prior knowledge. They have had diverse formal education experiences and are literate in one or more languages already. English can be a key to accessing additional training, becoming self-sufficient, advancing in a career, furthering their education, and improving themselves. It may be a way to expand their social networks and to integrate as members into a new academic or professional community.

This means that instructors should become aware of adults English learners' goals and needs for pursuing language learning and align instruction to help them effectively in meeting those needs and achieving those goals. The starting point for instruction is to recognize what tangible benefits adult learners are expecting to gain from knowing the language, because "knowing English" is likely a shorthand for working toward a goal that is beyond the mere acquisition of language skills. It means access to those areas of life—jobs, further training, and education—that require career-ready communication skills and proficiency in English. Consequently, the instruction that learners receive must be the kind that is truly useful for converting opportunity into reality.

What Adults Bring to Learning in ESP Settings

When designing instruction for occupational, professional, and academic purposes, teachers should start with what is known about adult learners. Understanding the characteristics of adult learners, particularly the strengths, skills, and knowledge that they already possess, gives teachers a foundation for designing instruction that connects with those assets and shows learners how to build on them to develop their English language skills and achieve their learning goals.

Every adult English learner is unique. ESP learners may come from a wide variety of different cultural, ethnic, or language backgrounds. They may differ in the quality and years of formal education they have received, and be accustomed to different traditions, cultural norms, religions, and ideologies. Each adult English learner brings a unique set of strengths and challenges, which are important for educators to know.

Adult learners have social capital. Adult English learners can derive resources from their colleagues and peers as well as from their larger social networks. The utility of their social capital differs by the resources available to their community, by the values and behaviors practiced within their networks, and by their proximity to their networks (EAP learners may be studying outside their countries of origin and thus have reduced contact with their networks, for example, whereas EPP learners may be in a course in their home country with culturally or linguistically similar peers, thus having access to their networks but also having reduced motivation to integrate with an English-speaking community). Therefore, learners' social capital may hinder or facilitate achievement of their learning goals (Zhou & Kim, 2006). How their network orients towards the use of English in everyday life bears on learners' motivation and on what resources they can generate to help them achieve those goals. When instructors are aware of each learner's social capital, they can encourage learners to draw on those resources, or they can explore with learners the difficulties that may require support from mentors in a new social network.

Adult learners set their own goals. Learners in ESP contexts typically have their own reasons for what and why they want to learn. They tend to weigh the value of participation in terms of "costs" (effort, time, self-esteem, and resources) versus "benefits" and frame their goals as social or economic (Appleby, 2010; Patterson, 2018). Their cost-benefit judgments are ongoing, and if they experience diminishing returns or slow progress toward their goals, or if they perceive the costs to be too high, they drop their studies. If adult English learners are to stay in programs long enough to acquire the skills they need, they must experience a direct connection between what they are learning and their personal or professional reasons for pursuing the program.

Adult English learners are developing their autonomy as learners. Although self-directed learning is developmentally desirable for most learners, not all adults possess the know-how for directing their own learning. Ways to support learners in developing autonomy include modeling, coaching, and explicit strategy instruction (Knowles, Holton, & Swanson, 2015; Merriam & Bierema, 2014). Instructors should encourage adult English learners to give their input about the course plan, the teaching approaches, and the evaluation of their own learning. The classroom atmosphere should emanate mutual respect, trust, and collaboration to foster a culture of self-directed learning.

Adult English learners have diverse life experiences and "funds of knowledge" to draw on. Adult learners are able to draw on their personal and professional experiences to reflect on and support their learning. For the most part, prior experiences provide a rich resource for mastering new skills and content (González, Moll, & Amanti, 2005). Within an EAP context, it can be particularly effective to encourage learners to share their knowledge within activities that compare and contrast aspects with their educational and social systems with the one in which they are studying. In a professional setting, learners usually have worked in a profession, but need to communicate and use that knowledge in English. Sharing professional knowledge and experience with their teachers and peers produces opportunities for authentic practice and meaningful applied learning.

> EPP learners usually have worked in a profession but need to communicate and use that knowledge in English. Sharing professional knowledge and experience with their teachers and peers produces opportunities for authentic practice and meaningful applied learning.

Adult English learners have linguistic capital. When learning a new language, ESP learners bring with them fully developed language ability in at least one language, or sometimes several languages. They have well-established neural pathways that make it possible for them to process that language automatically. They may also have conscious awareness of language structures in their previously learned languages. They can name thousands of concepts, carry out communicative functions with language, and use language to support a broad range of cognitive tasks. However, they vary in how much of their linguistic capital they can transfer to their new language. This depends on how much their other languages overlap with English in terms of the sound system, vocabulary, linguistic structures, and the writing system (National Research Council, 2012).

Adult English learners are resourceful with language usage. ESP learners are resourceful with how they apply their knowledge of languages. They are often able to switch dynamically between their languages in purposeful ways that reflect their awareness of another speaker's language repertoire as well as the full communicative context. This type of language behavior among bilinguals—known as translanguaging—serves as an expression of identity and group solidarity. Translanguaging can also be a very practical solution when individuals who are learning each other's languages try to communicate. For these reasons, translanguaging can play an instructional role when teachers encourage learners to convey meaning using the new language where they can and switch to another language in order to fill gaps (García, Johnson, & Seltzer, 2017).

How ESP Learners Learn Best

The strengths, skills, and knowledge that adult learners bring with them affect their approach to new learning. Adults learn best when their learning is relevant to their immediate needs and includes the problem solving and critical thinking that are part of adult functioning. Because adult learners only sustain learning that gives them a sense of growth and accomplishment (NASEM, 2018), designing the right kind of learning experiences and building on learner preferences are essential to promoting persistence.

For adults, learning happens both inside and outside of the classroom. Instructional time in the classroom is usually very limited relative to the learning goals most adult English learners identify, which makes spending it wisely critical. All adults, particularly those who are not used to formal classroom learning, can benefit from the guidance of a lifelong learning support system that will keep them moving toward achievement of their goals.

Adults learn best when they experience a pressing "need to know." Children, for the most part, learn a variety of subjects in school. Adults, however, have a pressing "need to know" as they ready themselves to take on specific new roles and assignments (Knowles, Holton, & Swanson, 2015; Merriam & Bierema, 2014). For example, seeking a new job, getting a job transfer, learning to drive, becoming a parent, buying a home, preparing taxes, applying for citizenship, and starting a business all create situations where the adult has an urgent need to learn quickly in order to apply knowledge right away. These changing roles and life tasks create authentic and compelling contexts for adult learning. In ESP contexts, the compelling nature of the "need to know" is heightened by its direct connection with adult English learners' ultimate goals for participation in specific professions, occupations, and academic fields.

Problem solving and critical thinking are at the core of all adult learning. Adults value troubleshooting and problem-solving skills. They want to make solid decisions based on understanding, questioning, making inferences, and evaluating information from various sources. Adults make important decisions daily for themselves and for others. The quality of their lives depends on having strong skills to support their decision-making. Teachers serve their learners best with language instruction that also includes critical thinking and problem-solving tasks at every proficiency level (Parrish & Johnson, 2010). In ESP contexts, adult English learners are motivated by instruction that poses critical thinking and problem-solving challenges relevant to their chosen academic or professional fields. For this reason, role plays and simulations are welcome techniques in ESP courses.

> Teachers serve their learners best with language instruction that also includes critical thinking and problem-solving tasks at every proficiency level.
> (Parrish & Johnson, 2010)

For many adults, learning informally can be as productive as classroom instruction. Much of what adults learn is not in classroom settings. Some adult learners have access to individual tutoring, online learning opportunities, and on-the-job apprenticing. Widening access to such options is important because they may fit the busy lifestyles of adults. Learning in non-classroom contexts can be more immediately applicable, which supports both motivation and the retention of new skills. Because classroom practice is usually limited to just a few hours per week, learning language is especially difficult if that learning is not extended outside the classroom. Therefore, helping adults access informal learning opportunities and teaching them strategies for extending their learning are vital components of educating them. This point is especially relevant for adult English learners in EAP, EPP, and EOP contexts, who will likely need to continue developing their English language proficiency after they transition to professional work and academic study.

The points outlined here draw on the extensive research on effective instruction for adult learners in many different types of educational and training settings. They are particularly pertinent for learners in EAP, EPP, and EOP settings because of the purpose-driven nature of both those learners and those types of programs.

Developing Language Proficiency for Academic and Other Specific Purposes

To develop English learners' language proficiency, teachers need to understand both the role of language in learners' goals and individual learning needs and the role of the English language in instruction. They must consider the differences among social, academic, professional and occupational language, as well as the characteristics of academic, professional, or occupational English. They may need to consult with different discourse communities to understand how to tailor their courses to their learners' needs and take account of standards that define English language proficiency for different contexts and purposes. In monitoring their learners' progress, teachers also need to consider research-based levels of language development and reasonable time frames for their learners to meet their learning objectives.

In academic settings, some EAP teachers were raised in English-speaking environments and attended school in places similar to those where their learners are headed, while others did not. Whatever experience they may hold as learners themselves, they cannot expect that all their learners will be able to follow teacher talk, ask questions, answer in intelligible speech, and participate in classroom discussions when they enroll in academic courses that are taught in English. Similarly, learners in EPP and EOP courses may have a range of educational and experiential backgrounds that differ from those of the instructors; they may be under pressure to obtain English language skills in a known field, or to develop knowledge of a new field in English rather than a language they already know. All EAP, EOP, and EPP instructors need to be aware of the role English will play in their learners' lives.

> Record 15 minutes of your own teaching, observe a university class or a communicative event in a workplace setting, or watch a video. Note how you (or the teacher or employee) and others rely on language to communicate meaning. What is the speaker saying, word for word? What language are the learners hearing and producing orally and/or in writing? In addition to language, in what other ways is meaning being conveyed? Reflect on the role of language in the segment.

Another thing that all ESP instructors have in common is that they cannot overlook the prominent role of language in their lessons. In addition to preparing learners for the types of language use that they will encounter when they move into their target academic, professional, or occupational settings, instructors must ensure that learners are able to understand the ways that English is used in their own teaching. For example, learners need specific vocabulary and skill sets in order to follow teacher instructions such as "read and summarize," "discuss with a partner," "take notes," "create a role play," and "fill in the blanks." Likewise, learners with differing educational backgrounds may have widely varying expectations for class activities and content; for example, they may expect a heavy focus on grammar exercises or resist participating in pair and small group work. Teachers need to be sensitive to differences in cultural background and educational experience, and develop common ground for beliefs and assumptions.

Effective teachers recognize that teaching linguistically diverse learners is a three-part challenge (see figure 2.1):

1. They must depart from predominantly language-based instruction and use a full repertoire of resources for meaning-making. These include pictorial, gestural, experiential, interactional, and linguistic supports.

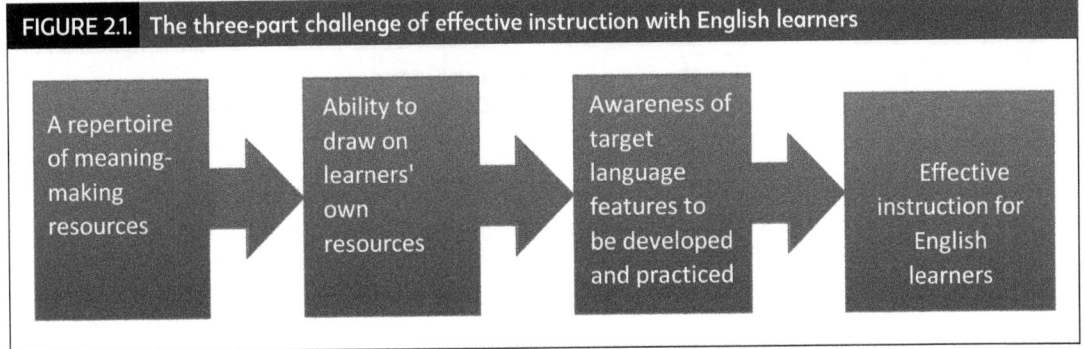

FIGURE 2.1. The three-part challenge of effective instruction with English learners

A repertoire of meaning-making resources → Ability to draw on learners' own resources → Awareness of target language features to be developed and practiced → Effective instruction for English learners

2. They need ways to help learners draw on their own available resources, such as linguistic, social, experiential, cognitive, procedural, and strategic knowledge.
3. They must become aware of the target language features that learners need to develop to be fully functional in the classroom or professional setting and with the specific content they are learning, and they need approaches to explicitly teach these target language forms at the same time that they are teaching their content.

Constantly monitoring learners' understanding and using instructional language to match their English language proficiency are hallmarks of high-quality teacher communication. Observing learners' language use at different proficiency levels demonstrates that all learners become more proficient with language over time. Effective teachers adjust to this development and match their own language use to the linguistic abilities of their learners, making sure to incrementally challenge learners to higher levels. Instructors need to be mindful of target language features and steer learners toward noticing, practicing, and using these features frequently in the classroom.

Characteristics of English in ESP Settings

Many EAP, EPP, and EOP learners can acquire the basic social language they need by actively engaging in communication, but this form of language acquisition is insufficient for most English learners in academic, professional, or occupational settings. EAP learners will need to learn the language of textbooks, informational texts, scholarly papers, instructional videos, academic presentations, and lectures. EPP learners will need to learn the language of professional written and oral communication in their fields of expertise, including that used in presentations, meetings, trade and professional publications, reports, and specifications. EOP learners must also develop language skills in their fields of expertise; these may include ability to read and write instructions, warnings, and other task-specific documents as well as ability to communicate effectively with coworkers, supervisors, and customers. In all cases, control of relevant English language skills is integral to a learner's academic, professional, or occupational success.

The task of acquiring a new language to the degree that one needs to succeed in that language is surprisingly lengthy and complex. Fully appreciating the complexity of this undertaking is difficult for anyone who has not tried to learn a new language. Table 2.1 displays the main characteristics of academic and professional/occupational language, at the conceptual, discourse, sentence, and word levels. To be considered proficient in the English of their specific context, learners need advanced levels in all four domains—listening, speaking, reading, and writing.

Table 2.1 Characteristics of proficient academic and professional/occupational English

Characteristic	Explanation of characteristic	Sentence Frames or Concepts	Examples in Context
Conceptual level			
Conceptual complexity	The treatment reflects cognitive functions: describing, explaining, comparing, classifying, sequencing, justifying, analyzing, evaluating, synthesizing.	This is what it looks like . . . This belongs in the category of . . . This is an important choice because . . . These . . . are related in this way.	This is what it looks like. The control panel has a temperature gauge. This belongs in the category of classical music, like Beethoven's sonatas. This is an important choice because it will affect all employees of the airline.
Development	Adequate details are provided. Claims are supported.	This means that . . . For example, . . . The sources of this information are . . .	This means that all employees will have access to healthcare benefits. Engineering has several subfields. For example, you can study electrical, mechanical, civil, or aeronautical engineering. The sources of this information are experts in the field.
Abstraction	Concrete events and objects are treated as representations of abstract concepts.	. . . is a key aspect of.	Expertise is a key aspect of professional identify.
Figurativeness	Abstract terms are assigned attributes of concrete things or live beings: they can move, communicate, or have intentions.	A . . . surfaced/was found. The . . . commands. . . The . . . was. . .	A problem has surfaced. The position commands respect. The analysis was incomplete.
Detachment	The speaker/writer separates from the message to suggest objectivity and logical reasoning.	Research shows that . . . The evidence points to . . .	Research shows that 4 out of 5 dentists believe that brushing teeth lessens the chances of cavities. The evidence points to the possibility of a new black hole in space.
Discourse level			
Organization	Ideas follow a logical progression. The topics are controlled. The connections between ideas are marked.	First . . . , second . . . , then . . . , finally . . . Nevertheless Consequently . . . , as a result . . .	First, shut off the electric current. Next remove the switch plate. Next carefully unscrew the junction box.

(continued)

Table 2.1 Characteristics of proficient academic and professional/occupational English *(continued)*

Characteristic	Explanation of characteristic	Sentence Frames or Concepts	Examples in Context
Discourse level *(continued)*			
Cohesion	Words and sentences are linked. Key words are repeated strategically. Pronouns match their referents.	On the one hand..., and on the other... Likewise... In contrast,... As mentioned above...	Visual representations can help us solve math problems. For example, a number line is one form of visual representation. It depicts a real number for each point.
Conciseness	Information is densely packed. Meanings may be nuanced.	Using fewer words, longer sentences, more embedded clauses and phrases, conjunctions and logical connectors	Currently, the annual mean growth rate of carbon dioxide in the Earth's atmosphere is 2.1 parts per million but is expected to increase.
Genre	The conventions of academic genres are observed.	Adjusting style to the genre's text features and conventions	Opinion essay, news article, journal article, interview, technical report, research report
Sentence level			
Precision	Sentences are complete, and each is formed with care. Qualifiers are frequent.	Using certainty or hedging as per the context; using specific terms instead of general ones.	It is mostly true. Results could improve. The best solution requires the fewest modifications to the blueprint.
Syntactic complexity	Phrase and sentence structures are varied and developed. Sentences are long.	Using a mix of simple, compound, complex, and compound-complex sentences.	It is true. We are working more than ever before to be able to afford the purchases we are choosing to make. And so, we are spending less time with the people who make our lives happy.
Density	Information is packed into elaborate noun phrases.	Using noun phrases with several modifiers, using synonyms and pronouns to refer to previously mentioned concepts	Several justifiable grievances against the released draft of the proposed technical manual were raised at the annual company meeting.
Grammar	Sentences adhere to the rules of formal grammar. Grammatical features that are less common in social language appear often.	Using lower-frequency vocabulary, passive voice, embedded clauses, modal auxiliaries, and a variety of verb tenses	The nurse queried the internist as to whom the medicine was for. Feedback should have been considered.
Mechanics	Error-free spelling and accurate punctuation	—	—

(continued)

Table 2.1 Characteristics of proficient academic and professional/occupational English *(continued)*

Characteristic	Explanation of characteristic	Sentence Frames or Concepts	Examples in Context
Word level			
Exactness	Words are intentionally selected from a set of vocabulary alternatives with regard to their frequency, connotations, and suitable collocates.	Using active verbs and specific/technical nouns	Alternatives for "goes down": happiness decreases; the price drops; the plane descends; stocks plummet
Conciseness	Ideas are condensed into technical terms. Extra words are omitted to avoid wordiness.	—	Climate agreement, protagonist, absolute value, parallelism Due to the fact that vs. because In the event that vs. if
Variety	Word repetition is avoided except for key words and for effect.	—	—
Clarity	The pronunciation of words reflects knowledge of sound patterns and word stress.	—	The White House v. a white house Bénefit, benefícial, beneficíary

(Adapted from TESOL, 2018, with material from Anstrom et al., 2010; Short & Echevarría, 2016; WIDA, 2012; Zwiers, 2014)

Shifting from Social to Academic/Professional Language

Learners who are learning English through informal communication tend to master social language first, much sooner than they can communicate in formal ways. Social language is typically conversational and requires mainly listening and speaking, with reading and writing of short or abbreviated messages such as texts and social media posts. Social language requires a vocabulary of only a few thousand high frequency words and the mastery of frequently heard utterance patterns. Learners' mastery of social language does not indicate proficiency in academic or professional language. In contrast, learners who learned English in non-English-speaking countries through grammar drills and academic reading are not likely to have had opportunities to engage in social English with native speakers, but may have some control of more formal academic or professional language.

The distinction between social language and academic or professional language is not binary. Development from less formal to more formal language unfolds along a continuum, with elements mastered gradually, over years of practice and instruction. In an age of social media and texting communication, ESP learners may be more experienced in social than academic or professional written communication. This may give EOP learners an advantage; much occupational English usage involves oral or written person-to-person communication between coworkers, with managers, and with customers or clients, so EOP learners can build on their existing skills with informal English to develop the occupation-focused vocabulary and communication skills that their learning goals entail. In academic and professional contexts, by contrast, learners' goals dictate the need to understand and produce longer spoken and written material that uses a greater range of vocabulary, including field-specific terminology, and complex discourse structures. In order to develop proficiency in academic or professional English, EAP and EPP learners need to master a range of genres and become able to adjust tone, style and register depending on the audience. However, all ESP learners, whether acquiring English for occupational, professional, or academic purposes, need explicit instruction to move communication from less formal English to the formal English they will need to achieve their goals.

The Continuum from Less Formal to More Formal Language in an EAP Context

A common concern of faculty members is the level of familiarity and social language used in email communication by EAP learners. Learners need to learn not only how to convey their message using appropriate salutations and language, but also what is and is not appropriate in communication with a professor.

Less Formal → More Formal and Professional	
Less Formal	Subject line: MISSED THE TEST!
	Hey Sir,
	I'm Mo from your stats class. Sorry, but I missed the test yesterday but my friend was sick and I had to take him to the hospital because he had BAD stomach cramps. He's okay, don't worry!! 😎
	See ya,
	Mo
	Subject line: Retake Stats Test?
	Hi. Prof. Johanssen,
	My name's Mo and I'm in your Introduction to Stats Class (STA 100) on Tuesday afternoons. I wasn't able to attend class last Tuesday because something happened. Can I retake it please? Thank you,
	Mo
	Subject line: Request STA 100 (Mohammed Yonis, 5557383)
	Dear Dr. Johanssen,
	I am in your Introduction to Stats Class (STA 100), Mohammed Yonis (Learner Number, 5557383). Due to an unexpected situation, I was unable to attend your class last Tuesday and unfortunately missed the test. I was wondering if you would grant me the opportunity to take the test during your next office hours. I apologize for my absence and the inconvenience it may cause.
More Formal and Professional	Sincerely,
	Mohammed Yonis

Language Development Through Use and Interaction

Effective teachers understand that language development involves active learning. Learners co-construct language; they learn to use language in the way that it is used when others communicate with them. Watching and overhearing speakers are not effective ways to learn a language. Rather, through conversation, learners establish joint attention with partners; they co-construct

> For ESP learners, English language competence is not an abstract skill or stored knowledge that may be useful someday in the future. It is functionality—the tool for shared cognition, shared understanding, and cooperation in relation to defined academic, professional, and occupational settings.

meaning, check their understanding, and ask for clarification. They can test their hypotheses about language forms and receive valuable, just-in-time feedback so they can make adjustments or learn something new (Mackey, Abbuhl, & Gass, 2012; Rex & Green, 2008; Swain & Suzuki, 2008).

The more frequent and varied learners' opportunities are to use language related to their target contexts, the more functional, complex, and flexible their language ability will become. This means that effective ESP teachers prompt learners to interact frequently, and they provide regular opportunities for learners to use language in varied modalities (listening, speaking, reading, writing) to complete tasks that mirror those that learners will encounter in academia and the professional world. Specific examples of how teachers promote language use in the classroom include the following:

Teacher-centered practices to promote language use:

- Providing language frames and language models so that learners can learn to articulate language functions (for example, they know what expressions to use if they want to agree or disagree, build on another person's idea, or explain a process)
- Asking learners to notice language forms in texts and to make use of them in their oral and written discourse
- Preparing a glossary of key subject-specific or technical terms
- Creating a class webpage or Padlet with resources for language learning and for the content being studied through English

Learner-centered practices to promote language use:

- Grouping learners to compare, share, and discuss ideas and plans before they start a writing task
- Developing role plays and simulations to engage learners in practical applications of the language
- Using peer review and other peer-feedback practices

In short, effective teachers multiply opportunities for learners' active engagement with the English language skills and modalities that are most relevant to their target academic, occupational, and professional settings.

Language Development through Reading and Writing

To achieve competence in the English they must have to achieve their occupational, professional, or academic goals, ESP learners need practice with relevant reading and writing skills and materials. Breadth and depth of vocabulary and the full mastery of language forms can be achieved only by engaging with formal written and recorded texts. To develop such English proficiency, ESP learners must engage in extensive and intensive reading. Extensive reading, often with learners reading on their own, will have a beneficial effect on language proficiency because it ensures that they encounter a wide range of vocabulary and language forms (Hafiz & Tudor, 1989; Macalister, 2008). Intensive reading is usually supported by the teacher and provides opportunities for building depth of knowledge of target words and linguistic forms.

As instructors help strengthen the reading and writing skills of their adult English learners, they need to be aware of possible challenges to the process, such as an unfamiliar writing system, confusing and inconsistent spelling rules, a need for oral language connections, a lack of vocabulary knowledge, low motivation to read, and a lack of background knowledge.

Working with an unfamiliar writing system. English learners vary in their knowledge of the English writing system, particularly if their native language uses an entirely different form of writing. Writing systems vary in the linguistic features of the language that they mark, such as vowel or consonant sounds, sound length, tone, or stress. Writing scripts vary from alphabetic (such as English, Russian, Greek, Korean) to consonants only (Arabic, Hebrew) to syllabic (Bengali, Gujarati, Thai) and logographic (Mandarin). Harder than mastering the script itself is learning the specific language features that a writing system encodes. The writing system of English, for example, demands attention to both consonant and vowel sounds but not to word stress, consonant length, or tone (Borgwaldt & Joyce, 2013; Weingarten, 2013).

Dealing with confusing spelling rules. Because pronunciation often does not match spelling in English, adult English learners may struggle when reading and writing. Consider the spelling variations for sounds that are the same (y*ou*, d*o*, thr*ew*, thr*ough*, sh*oe*, *ewe*, q*ueue*, fl*u*, tr*ue*). English has many dialects in which pronunciation is systematically different and the spelling of words may also differ depending on where one is learning English. The alphabet is a very small part of learning to read in English, in contrast to the much larger part that it plays in those languages where the sound-letter correspondence is more predictable. Instructors can guide learners in strategies for using a spellchecker effectively or asking a colleague to proofread their text.

Building background knowledge and using oral language skills to support reading comprehension. Background knowledge refers to the information and conceptual understandings or schemas that readers bring to their comprehension of texts. Studies have shown that second language learners' content familiarity can partly compensate for linguistic knowledge at most proficiency levels. Conversely, lack of schema and relevant background knowledge will impede reading comprehension even for advanced language learners. However, oral language serves as a scaffold for reading. Teachers can help learners develop background knowledge about key concepts in a text they will read through discussion, vocabulary development, video clips, and other supports. In EPP and EOP contexts, where instructors may not be familiar with the content and concepts of learners' target occupations and professions, they can involve learners in the process of surfacing the relevant background knowledge, using translanguaging strategies as needed to build mutual understanding in English. When teachers talk with learners about the content of texts before and after reading, they promote both oral language skills and reading comprehension (Baker et al., 2014; Grabe, 2009; Krekeler, 2006; Saunders & O'Brian, 2006.)

Coping with unknown words. Research indicates that comprehension of text read independently depends in large part on how many words a reader knows in the text (Nagy & Scott, 2000). For example, knowing 80 percent of words in a text might seem reasonable; yet, reading comprehension is virtually impossible at 80 percent of vocabulary coverage. For minimal reading comprehension, a reader should know 90 percent of the words, and for adequate comprehension and to learn content information, 95 percent. For unassisted reading for pleasure—the most sustainable and rewarding reading activity—most readers should have 98 percent vocabulary coverage (Nation & Webb, 2011; Schmitt, Jiang, & Grabe, 2011). These facts have important implications for teachers of ESP learners.

The Types of Words to Learn

- High frequency words. The 2,800 most-frequent word families cover 90 percent of all that is spoken and written in English. A current source for this vocabulary is the New General Service List (www.newgeneralservicelist.org).
- General academic words. Some academic vocabulary is less subject-specific. These terms are cross-curricular and thus useful in every discipline. A current source is the New Academic Word List (http://www.newacademicwordlist.org/), which contains 960 headwords.
- Content vocabulary commonly used in academic content areas or specific workplace settings. These terms are specific to a content area (such as that used in a university course) or a profession.

Managing texts that are too difficult. Some readings that ESP learners have to manage are above their English reading proficiency levels, yet they need ways to make sense of them. Learners need to draw on their reading skills and comprehension strategies to decode meaning. Effective teachers forecast the challenges that learners may have with complicated texts and scaffold vocabulary building through pre-activities. They also plan tasks to strengthen the learners' metacognitive and cognitive strategy usage (e.g., making predictions, monitoring understanding, annotating, making inferences, summarizing, generalizing). Further, when teachers know what learners are knowledgeable and passionate about, they can direct them to texts where their prior experiences and existing background information support reading comprehension and bootstrap language learning.

Conditions for Second Language Learning

Every teacher would like to know the best way to teach a second language to any learner. However, although an entire field of research—second language acquisition—is dedicated to examining this topic, no one has yet provided a definitive answer. A dozen theories focus on the neurological, psychological, cognitive, and/or linguistic processes by which people learn languages other than their first or native one.

Despite the range of theories, language education professionals have learned from decades of research findings that some conditions are essential, and some conditions are beneficial for second language acquisition. Some individual variables play a role, too.

Essential Conditions

Essential conditions are those that must be present for second language acquisition to occur. Teachers can play a role in promoting some of these. Essential conditions include the following:

Neurophysiological capacity. Language is a complex neurophysiological function. It can be thought of as software that runs on the hardware of the brain (Anderson & Lightfoot, 2002). Second language acquisition is facilitated by the software of the first language. In other words, a learner's acquisition of his or her home language establishes neurophysiological processing that plays a key role in how he or she handles input in a new language. Normal first language development indicates that all is well with the learner's neurophysiology for acquiring additional languages.

Motivation. Motivation is the force that prompts individuals to pursue and sustain an effort toward a goal. Language learning requires a great deal of effort over a period of many years. Activities that lead to language learning must be inherently pleasurable or the eventual goals must be so positive that they are worth the struggle. Within academic and other specific learning contexts, not all learners may be highly motivated to learn English, as learning English may be imposed on them by their parents, in the case of an EAP learner, or by an employer, in the case of an EOP or EPP learner. Therefore, instructors should work with each learner to understand and optimize internal sources of motivation (Dörnyei & Ushioda, 2011). Effective teachers explain the connection between the objectives of a lesson or course and how the task is related to their learners' learning goals.

> In EAP programs, many learners are focused on passing standardized language tests, such as IELTS or TOEFL, to meet their admission requirements. Teachers however may focus on providing a toolbox of skills and strategies to facilitate the academic work their learners will encounter in their university studies. Teachers need to zoom in and out of the short-term and long-term motivations of their learners and adapt their lessons accordingly.

Facilitative emotional conditions. Learning cannot succeed if learners are anxious, worried, or feel overwhelmed. Under negative emotional conditions, the learner shuts down and is unable to take risks with language or attend to language forms. In contrast, a welcoming, safe, and relaxed environment is indispensable for language learning. Managing emotions and supporting each learner to overcome anxieties or negative emotional responses are essential teaching responsibilities (Williams, Mercer, & Ryan, 2015).

Usable input and feedback. Input can refer to how teachers present information. The term is also related to *comprehensible input*, which denotes language that is slightly above the language level that the learner already knows (Krashen, 1985). Input beyond a learner's understanding can become usable when a teacher scaffolds the learning to support meaning through other means, such as visual aids, gestures, learner experiences, and the like. Another form of input that is key to acquisition is feedback. Without feedback, learners cannot be certain that the language they produce is understandable in its meaning, form, or pronunciation. A large body of research exists on the many useful varieties and relative efficacy of different types of teacher feedback (Ellis, 2017; Ellis & Shintani, 2014; Lyster & Saito, 2010; Nassaji & Kartchava, 2017). Some types of feedback are clarification requests, explicit correction, reformulations, metalinguistic signals, and recasts. Prompting speakers to repair their own speech, also called elicitation of self-repair, is a highly effective practice to motivate learners in becoming autonomous.

> *Dave teaches English for technologists at a small technical college in La Paz, Bolivia. The undergraduate program has recognized that many engineers experience difficulty in communicating their ideas effectively to a team or a manager. Therefore, the main learning outcome in Dave's high-intermediate course is for the learners to co-present their end-of-term team project with fluency and accuracy. Dave understands that not all oral feedback is noticed by his learners, so at the beginning of the term, Dave explicitly explains the feedback types he will be using to correct his learners. He models different examples of feedback and does some in-class paired exercises for learners to notice feedback and self-repair. As the end of term approaches, he has the teams rehearse their presentations in class and provides feedback.*

Deliberate practice. Practice is the collective name for activities whose goal is to systematically develop second language skills (DeKeyser, 2007, 2010). These activities are not drills that demand imitation and repetition; rather, practice is a much broader range of activities that lead to fluency, accuracy, and automaticity of specific sub-skills. Knowing language rules cognitively is not the same as applying them in real time, fluently, consistently, and without conscious awareness. Language proficiency involves moving focused attention on basic skills into accurately executed, automatic processes. Mastering a second language requires a complex set of skills that take thousands of hours of systematic, deliberate practice to develop (DeKeyser, 2007, 2010).

The foundation of effective instruction is monitoring and ensuring that all of the essential conditions for second language acquisition are met and sustained for every learner. Instructors in EOP, EPP, and EAP courses can promote motivation and facilitative emotional conditions by recognizing their adult English learners' learning goals, understanding the challenges that may be impeding goal achievement, and showing learners how various learning activities incorporate the goals and provide strategies and skills for overcoming the impediments.

Beneficial Conditions

Beneficial conditions are those conditions that contribute to second language learning and work to the advantage of learners who have access to them. Some beneficial conditions depend on the context of language learning, while others can be enhanced by instructional practices.

Relatedness of first and new languages. Saying that the first language is "closer to" the new language—in this case English—means that the first language and the new language have similar speech sounds and phonological features, have many cognates (words that have similar form and meaning), have the same basic word order, and use the same writing system. In such cases, learning a new language is significantly easier. Learning a new language that is quite different from the first language, such as learning English when the first language is Bengali, is harder and typically takes longer.

Avid reading. Being a motivated, avid reader in a first language helps in acquiring an additional one. Practiced readers decode words automatically. They are able to hold their focus on texts for long periods of time. These skills are preliminary for being able to allocate working memory to the task of word learning by not struggling with the decoding task. Avid readers also read more; this means that they encounter more words and meet each word more frequently, which can result in a larger vocabulary and deeper word knowledge. Skilled readers, such as those in EPP and EAP programs, have developed reading comprehension strategies in the first language, such as inferring the meaning of new words from context or quickly identifying main ideas and supporting details, that they can transfer to the new one (Grabe, 2009).

Prior foreign language learning. If a learner has experience learning a foreign language or is bilingual, learning English will be easier. Bilinguals bring to the learning process prior experiences, self-efficacy, and strategies that helped them succeed previously (De Angelis, 2007; Ó Laoire & Singleton, 2009). They are able to draw on the language that they consider to be closer to the target language. They do not necessarily "understand" the differences between the language (or languages) that they speak and the new language, but they draw effectively on their intuition, and they are ready to "give it a go" (Rutgers & Evans, 2015).

Cultural knowledge and the ability to read social situations. Language and culture are intricately bound together; communication depends on gleaning meaning from contexts and assumptions and on being attuned to nonverbal cues. Being able to process situations, gestures, or unarticulated intentions correctly is important for inferring the real meaning of messages (Lynch, 2011). ESP learners who already understand the cultural differences between their target academic, professional, or occupational contexts and those with which they are more familiar, or have teachers who serve in the role of culture facilitator, are at an advantage.

> *Xia is a UX designer at an agency in Shanghai who has recently been assigned to an international team to develop an app for learning. Xia's first thought after being assigned the project was that she would experience difficulty in being understood by her remote team. As a result, she teleconferences with her remote team on a weekly basis. Seeing her colleagues' faces on the screen not only helps her better understand the intended meaning of her colleagues, but also facilitates her own communication because she can use facial and other gestures to get her points across.*

Personality factors. Research has identified a number of personality factors as facilitative for language learning, such as courage (shaking off fear, being willing to take risks), positivity (reacting with positive emotional responses to experiences), tolerance for ambiguity (experiencing partial understandings as "the glass half full"), and willingness to communicate in specific situations (Brown & Larson-Hall, 2012; Williams, Mercer, & Ryan, 2015).

Regular access to competent speakers of the new language. Although all types of interaction are useful for language learning, learners gain more from interacting with teachers, employers, coworkers, and proficient peers (Sato & Ballinger, 2016). Sometimes teachers assume that learners have access to interaction with native speakers if they live in an English-speaking country; however, this is not always the case. Each learner's circumstances are different. Teachers can encourage this type of interaction outside of the course.

Having purposes and frequent opportunities to use the new language. Having reasons and occasions to use the new language is closely related to the previous condition of having access to competent speakers. But this condition matters even more than that one for language learning. It is also an achievable condition within most instructional contexts with careful lesson planning. Regardless of the educational context, lessons with collaborative learning tasks such as pair work, small-group work, and one-on-one coaching benefit most learners.

Integrative motivation. This is one type of motivation that deserves separate mention from motivation for language learning in general (Gardner, 1985). In addition to instrumental motivation, such as wanting to improve job prospects or wanting to be able to manage university studies in English, ESP learners may be motivated by the desire to be or become part of an English-speaking academic or professional community. This integrative motivation will cause them to work harder (Pavlenko & Norton, 2007). For example, English learners studying in a university intensive English program (IEP) may want to become involved in extracurricular activities conducted in English; English learners in an EOP course may want to be able to participate in staff lunchroom interactions.

Effective instruction includes all the necessary conditions of second language acquisition, leverages beneficial conditions, and mitigates the challenging factors for language learning (NASEM, 2017). Chapter 3 offers a wealth of ideas for providing high-quality instruction that facilitates learning academic and occupational English.

Additional Factors

Most of the conditions discussed so far are within a teacher's or learner's control and can enhance language learning. Three additional factors merit consideration. These factors potentially affect second language learning, so teachers should recognize them and try to minimize their impact with specialized instruction and suitable interventions.

Older learners. The age at which a learner's exposure to the new language begins matters for the eventual outcome of language learning. Ample evidence suggests that there are some limits on post-adolescent development of native-like proficiency, particularly regarding pronunciation. Nonetheless, advanced proficiency and dynamic bilingualism are achievable for these learners (Birdsong, 2016; DeKeyser, 2013; Muñoz, 2011). In all ESP contexts, a significant number of participants may be "older" (that is, beyond the usual age range for postsecondary or graduate work). These learners may believe that they will not be able to develop their desired proficiency levels in English due to their age. Effective ESP instructors address this fear directly and provide examples and strategies to build these learners' confidence in their potential. These instructors also guard against allowing a given learner's age to influence their own expectations.

Learner expectations for progress. Adult English learners are often unaware of how long it takes to develop English language proficiency to a level that allows them to achieve the goal of functioning on a par with proficient English-speaking peers. They do not expect to participate in an English language development program for many years, and this mismatch of expectations and reality can lead to tension and disappointment. Adults come to language programs to meet their needs. The resources they require in order to participate are many, and they generally cannot sustain years of attendance. The best approach for instructors in ESP contexts is to inform learners about the time needed to achieve their goals, offer them (as quickly as possible) language skills they can put to immediate use, and equip them with useful tools and strategies so they can continue their learning independently outside the classroom.

Socioemotional factors and special needs. The challenges that socioemotional factors present to second language learning can manifest themselves in many forms, including trauma, post-traumatic stress, anxiety, depression, speech and language disorders, and learning disabilities. Effective teachers actively screen and monitor for these, advocate for learners, and engage specialists if possible without relinquishing their own responsibilities to support every learner's learning within their own classroom. The recommended approach is to use multi-tiered, evidence-based interventions that are culturally and linguistically responsive (Hoover, Baca, & Klinger, 2016; NASEM, 2017).

When teachers pair their understanding of the conditions for second language learning with knowledge of each adult English learner's learning goals, background, educational history, and personal characteristics, they can maximize the conditions that they control or shape. However, even when all essential and beneficial conditions are met, instructors must understand that not all adult English learners are driven to become proficient speakers, readers or writers of English. For some, being able to develop specialized vocabulary and perform specific communication tasks may be enough. Acquiring proficiency in English, and, specifically in academic or professional English, is an involved, long-term enterprise, which takes years of instruction and deliberate practice. Whether a learner is striving to be a proficient speaker of English or to perform effectively in certain tasks, each learner is worthy of every teacher's support. Teachers preparing lessons for their learners need to refer to their needs analyses and goal statements, and design instruction to help each learner meet individual learning objectives. Chapter 3 explains in detail the process of designing instruction to optimize essential and beneficial conditions of second language acquisition and to limit the challenging factors to the extent possible within a specific teaching context.

> Review the list of essential and beneficial conditions as well as additional factors that may affect second language learning in ESP contexts. Which do you consider when you are planning instruction? What could you do to give your ESP learners a greater advantage in language development?

English Language Proficiency Levels

The development of language is continuous, incremental, and unnoticed except during or following periodic growth spurts. For the purposes of instruction and assessment, experts have described what language use typically looks like or sounds like at every level for each of the four language modalities (listening, speaking, reading, and writing).

However, it is important to realize that language development is not steady or inevitable along trajectories, nor is it balanced across the four language modalities. Some learners show evidence of language gains in bursts, whereas others plateau, especially in the absence of regular interaction with proficient speakers and beneficial feedback. And, of course, much of language development is latent, taking place in the mind, and is often difficult to characterize in terms of observable language use. With careful attention, teachers can learn to recognize the markers that indicate language development:

- Increased length of utterances (oral or written phrases and sentences)
- Greater variety of utterance patterns
- Broader choice of words, including words of increased specificity, and greater awareness of their appropriateness to convey intended meaning
- Increased comprehensibility of the ideas being communicated
- Increased appropriateness of the level of formality (register) to audience and occasion
- Decreased use of hesitation phenomena (*ah, hm, er*)
- Reduced use of filler expressions (*stuff like that, you know*) and formulaic phrases
- Increased use of cultural referents

Learners who rely on sentence fragments, repetitive structures, and formulaic expressions are usually less proficient than those who produce a lot of detail and variety in their language, who choose their words carefully, and who can change the way in which they express themselves, depending on the conversation partner or communicative situation.

Following are basic descriptions of the levels of English language proficiency that are generally recognized in the field. These can help teachers identify the current levels of their learners, but they are relatively simple in comparison to the detailed standards documents teachers have available to guide their instruction.

Beginner Levels
At the beginner levels, learners typically rely on context to interpret meaning; they manage short and simple texts about familiar topics. They perform concrete tasks and communicate basic messages. They produce short phrases and sentences with repetitive patterns. They possess a small vocabulary, which consists of high-frequency words and memorized chunks of language. High beginners can understand and form longer phrases and sentences that connect ideas. Their vocabulary grows to several thousand words, which allows them to begin reading abridged texts that contain a clear organization and controlled vocabulary.

Intermediate Levels
Intermediate learners can succeed in reading texts that have a clear structure and familiar contexts, and that contain a broader range of vocabulary, that is, a few thousand words. Intermediate learners can handle conversations about most topics related to their daily life and work. When listening to others, they can identify the main topic and important details of a conversation. They can perform tasks with familiar steps. They are able to gather information to learn about new topics, and they can write a simple paragraph about a familiar matter, which contains a main idea and supporting details. At the high-intermediate stage, learners can manage a range of texts independently. They can read for different purposes. They are able to participate in a variety of social interactions and express themselves in multiple, related sentences. Intermediate learners can provide explanations, descriptions, and comparisons. Their accuracy and fluency with language is improving, as is their ability to produce a wider variety of sentence patterns.

Advanced Levels
Advanced learners easily manage routine texts, even ones that contain some technical and specialized vocabulary. They know enough words to independently read unabridged texts of lesser complexity. They still have difficulty with idioms, fixed expressions, and figurative language. They can formulate a reasoned argument, explain a position, and cite textual evidence. They can write a report about a problem or construct a basic position essay or a work-related policy recommendation. Their writing demonstrates coherence and growing accuracy with a broad range of

grammatical forms. They show awareness of the audience by switching register as appropriate. They can converse naturally and fluently about most topics.

Proficient Levels

Proficient individuals can handle complex texts across a wide range of subjects. They can analyze and critically evaluate the reasoning of writers and speakers. They can write out a detailed explanation or a reasoned argument and carry out a research project to gain new knowledge. In their writing, they can treat abstract topics by explaining, evaluating, and synthesizing information. They can explicate information from graphs and data tables. They can edit and proofread their writing because they have good control of the subtleties of grammar, idiomatic expressions, register, and genre. Proficient individuals can express themselves at length in clear, fluent speech, and they can participate in formal discussions on complex issues. They are able to carry out higher-order tasks such as negotiating and persuading others.

Most EAP programs aim for advanced or proficient levels of English due to the motivation of the learner to engage in an academic setting. The success of the learner in this context is based on an advanced knowledge of English. For EOP and EPP programs, the initial needs assessment, particularly the interviews with stakeholders such as managers and colleagues, is essential for identifying the proficiency levels that learners will need in each of the four modalities in order to carry out work-related tasks effectively.

It is worth emphasizing, however, that in all areas of ESP, learners will inevitably focus on language proficiency in their specific domains or disciplines. All learners in a given EAP class may need to attend lectures or write research papers, for example, but, as detailed in Chapter 1, engineering students use language in very different ways from medical students, and being proficient in one area does not imply proficiency in another. Similarly, learners in other areas of ESP will focus on their own requirements. Hospitality staff in a five-star hotel will never need to master the skills of writing academic articles, and likewise, university students will not have to master the language of the professional event planner. In ESP courses, language proficiency is always domain-specific and always interacts with subject knowledge. Sometimes this means that learners are proficient in a particular skill or area even when their general English skills are low.

Standards for Second Language Learning

Standards play a role in all types of ESP courses for several reasons. For one, they guide the development of standardized tests and commercially produced materials. A learner of academic English usually has to reach a certain score on a standardized test as proof of proficiency for university or college admission. Similarly, some learners in EOP and EPP courses have to show proof of their language proficiency level to their employers. Therefore, academic, professional, and occupational English programs refer to standards to determine their curricular outcomes, materials, placement, and assessment tools.

Standards also set widely accepted benchmarks of learning. Levels of proficiency determined by national and international standards can give teachers a more transparent and cohesive understanding of the ability of the learner. So, instructors in ESP contexts, particularly those that enroll learners from many countries, need to understand the English language education standards and tests that other countries use. In general, tests based on these standards measure test takers' performance with listening, speaking, reading, and writing in English, and employ progressively complex texts and tasks. These assessments start with the more practical and contextually supported tasks and move toward more abstract and cognitively demanding ones.

Some standards include "can-do" competencies and descriptors that configure the four language modalities into broader categories such as reception, production, interaction and mediation (e.g., American Council on the Teaching of Foreign Languages, 2010; Council of Europe, 2018). These configurations align language skills with the types of communicative tasks that are relevant for academic, professional, and occupational learning contexts. More information can be found in the documents listed in Table 2.2.

Table 2.2 Common English language standards used in ESP		
Standards document	Levels	Reference
Common European Framework of Reference (CEFR)	6 levels: Basic User A1–A2, Independent User B1–B2, Proficient User C1–C2	Council of Europe, 2018
Canadian Language Benchmarks	12 levels: Beginner to Intermediate CLB 1–4, Advanced CLB 5–8, Proficient CLB 9–12	Centre for Canadian Language Benchmarks, 2012
Global Scale of English	Extends CEFR with a mastery scale from 10 to 90 for the skills within CEFR levels	Pearson English, n.d.
Australian Core Skills Framework	4 levels: Beginner ACSF Level 1, Intermediate ACSF Level 2, Advanced ACSF Level 3, Proficient ACSF Level 4	Australian Government Department of Education and Training, 2015
American Council on the Teaching of Foreign Languages (ACTFL) Proficiency Guidelines	4 levels: Novice (low, mid, high), Intermediate (low, mid, high), Advanced (low, mid, high), Superior	ACTFL, 2012

The Role of Language in Identity

Instructors must always remember to consider each learner as an individual. The way in which each learner uses language is personal, and identity is delicately wrapped in how one speaks and interacts with others (Dörnyei, 2014; Douglas Fir Group, 2016; Norton, 2013; Ushioda, 2009). Each person is easily recognized by voice, the characteristic intonation of speech, particular speech habits, and accent. How individuals relate to their language use is important for their notions of self-worth and their academic and professional careers. It affects any potential relationships that they establish.

Knowing two or more languages is a strength. Teachers in EPP, EOP, and EAP contexts are culturally responsive educators who recognize that adult English learners are well positioned to become proficient in more than one language, and the optimal long-term outcome for these learners is dynamic bilingualism. Dynamic bilingualism is the ability to adapt to communicative situations and use more than one language flexibly and strategically to make meaning, depending on the audience, conversation partner, or topic (García, Ibarra Johnson, & Seltzer, 2017).

The goal for all ESP learners is to obtain communicative competence in English for their target situation. Dynamic bilinguals are fully functional with communicative partners who use either or both of their languages. They can cross linguistic and cultural boundaries with ease, and they can participate in knowledge communities beyond these borders.

Effective ESP instructors recognize that identity is dynamic. It can be shaped and formed by discourse communities; in turn, membership in such communities motivates learners to

> One language sets you in a corridor for life. Two languages open every door along the way.
> —Frank Smith

communicate in the ways valued by those groups. Integrating and including learners in the discourse community shapes their identity and motivation to realize their ideal self.

A Look Back and a Look Ahead

Chapter 2 has presented foundational information about second language learning. The chapter has highlighted the following ideas:

- The English language has a prominent role in instruction for academic, professional, and occupational purposes.
- Adult English learners can learn content by multimodal means, and they bring their own pre-existing resources for learning to the courses as well. EPP, EOP, and EAP learners are motivated, have goals for language learning, and are self-directed.
- The development of English language proficiency entails the control and length of utterances, the growth of vocabulary, and the mastery of language functions and registers. Academic, professional, and occupational English are important varieties of the English language that require mastery of listening, speaking, reading, and writing skills.
- Not all learners have the same challenges. It is easier to learn a new language if you have learned one before, if your first language is similar to English, and if you are literate in your first language.
- Successful second language acquisition depends on five essential conditions: neurophysiological capacity, motivation, facilitative emotional conditions, usable input and feedback, and deliberate practice. Effective instruction guarantees that these factors are in place and also incorporates beneficial conditions, which include frequent interaction, avid reading, skills transfer from first language, and integrative motivation.
- High-quality ESP instruction maximizes comprehensible input for learners by building on the language that learners already know, by giving appropriate feedback frequently, and by scaffolding learners' comprehension with multi-modal input. Teachers promote motivation in the classroom by supporting learner collaboration in a language-learning environment.

Chapter 3 fleshes out The 6 Principles that undergird exemplary teaching of English learners:

1. Know your learners.
2. Create conditions for language learning.
3. Design high-quality lessons for language development.
4. Adapt lesson delivery as needed.
5. Monitor and assess learner language development.
6. Engage and collaborate within a community of practice.

As you read that chapter and explore The 6 Principles and related practices, apply the ideas about second language acquisition that Chapter 2 has presented. The 6 Principles derive from research-based understandings about how language develops. Let those understandings about language acquisition serve as an essential backdrop as you move through Chapter 3.

Also reflect on your own practice as you read the next chapter.

- Consider what you know about your learners and which aspects of their backgrounds may influence their second language development (Principle 1).
- Reflect on how you organize your courses and bolster positive conditions for language development. Do you make sure you are preparing lessons that are relevant to the learners' professional and academic goals and linguistic needs? (Principle 2).

- Evaluate how you keep learners' language proficiency levels in mind when you are planning and delivering lessons. Think about the ways in which you convey content knowledge. Do you use a large repertoire of nonlinguistic resources and embed mini-lessons of key English language functions and forms that are especially useful for learning the content that you teach? Do you frequently incorporate tasks that require learners to interact and use language in authentic tasks? (Principle 3).
- Reflect on what happens while you are implementing your lesson, and how you make necessary adjustments through differentiation, scaffolding, or background building to improve learner comprehension or task performance (Principle 4).
- Also consider how you go about continually monitoring your learners' output of language, whether it be oral or written, on target task, assignment or a summative assessment, to be sure that your learners are making timely progress in their language development (Principle 5).
- Finally, reflect on how you continually develop and strengthen your teaching through collaboration within a community of practice (Principle 6).

Additional resources for this book are available at www.the6principles.org/eap-esp.

3 TEACHING WITH THE 6 PRINCIPLES FOR ACADEMIC AND OTHER SPECIFIC PURPOSES

As noted in the previous chapters, English is taught as a second or foreign language around the world to a wide variety of adult learners, including those focused on ESP (English for specific purposes). These English learners can study in a variety of settings; for example, they may be at colleges and universities, or in PLIs (private language institutes) or IEPs (intensive English programs) held in any number of locations. They may be studying through a corporate training department, or they may be learning on the job. These English learners have many different needs, abilities, and goals, and they vary in cultural and language background, situation, and English level. Some may already be matriculated into a college or university in an English-speaking setting; others may be in an IEP preparing for academic pursuits. Still others may be pursuing a certain career path, such as nursing, aviation, or law. Their needs vary as well, with some needing study in reading, writing, listening, speaking, grammar, and vocabulary and others needing mostly oral communication. What most of these learners share is the need for more instructional support in the skill areas to prepare them to meet their individual academic or professional goals.

As detailed in Chapter 2, adults who have learned their native language can learn a new language, but doing so takes time, persistence, and deliberate, ongoing practice. These same requirements apply to adult English learners who want to gain language proficiency for personal or professional reasons. Learners need frequent opportunities to work with appropriate content so they can test and develop their English in relation to the expectations and requirements of their target performance or proficiency. Practice needs to be suitable in terms of level and content so that learners can transition to the next stage.

Teachers face multiple challenges in elevating learners to levels that will allow them to survive and thrive in English in the workplace or the academic classroom. In an EAP (English for academic purposes) context, English learners often are not adequately prepared for the rigors of academic, content-based material and the expectations for class participation, particularly in upper-level courses. Similarly, in EOP (English for occupational purposes) and EPP (English for professional purposes) settings, learners may require support in developing understanding of relevant cultural norms and commonly used procedures. In all cases, learners may be unprepared to meet expectations for team and group work, managing miscommunication and asking for clarification, or working with proficient speakers of English who will be their advisors, professors, supervisors, and colleagues.

Despite these challenges, experienced teachers have achieved excellence by following key principles for effective ESP instruction. This chapter describes each of The 6 Principles and identifies practices that are helpful for implementing and supporting each one. The chapter also presents examples that flesh out the practices and illustrates how teachers in ESP courses may implement them.

The 6 Principles for Exemplary Teaching of English Learners and Recommended Practices

1. **Know your learners.**
   1a. Teachers gain information about their learners.
   1b. Teachers embrace and leverage the resources that learners bring to the classroom to enhance learning.

2. **Create conditions for language learning.**
   2a. Teachers promote a supportive learning environment, with attention to reducing learners' anxiety and developing trust.
   2b. Teachers demonstrate expectations of success for all learners.
   2c. Teachers plan instruction to enhance and support learners' motivation for language learning.

3. **Design high-quality lessons for language development.**
   3a. Teachers prepare lessons with clear outcomes and convey them to their learners.
   3b. Teachers provide and enhance input through varied approaches, techniques, and modalities.
   3c. Teachers engage learners in the use and practice of authentic language and materials.
   3d. Teachers design lessons so that learners engage with relevant and meaningful content.
   3e. Teachers plan differentiated instruction according to their learners' English language proficiency levels, literacy levels, needs, and goals.
   3f. Teachers promote the use of learning strategies, problem solving skills, and critical thinking.
   3g. Teachers promote self-directed learning.

4. **Adapt lesson delivery as needed.**
   4a. Teachers check comprehension frequently and adjust instruction according to learner responses.
   4b. Teachers adjust their talk, the task, or the materials according to learner responses.

5. **Monitor and assess learners' language development.**
   5a. Teachers monitor learner errors.
   5b. Teachers provide ongoing feedback effectively and strategically.
   5c. Teachers use effective formative and summative assessment strategies.

6. **Engage and collaborate within a community of practice.**
   6a. Teachers are fully engaged in their profession.
   6b. Teachers coordinate and collaborate with colleagues.

Principle 1. Know Your Learners

Michael Williams has just accepted a job as an EAP instructor at an IEP at a university in the United States. He is not a new teacher, but this is his first position teaching in a university setting. The learners are not yet matriculated into university courses; Michael's job is to prepare them for classes at the university. On the first day of class, he has the learners complete the same profile sheet that he often uses and keeps with his file for each learner. He asks for information such as

- *Name (pronunciation and spelling)*
- *Nickname*
- *Native Country and Language*
- *Email Address (or other contact information)*
- *Length of Time Studying/Speaking English*
- *TOEFL Scores (and other placement test or standardized test information)*

When he gets to his office, he begins to plan his lessons for the first few weeks of his Advanced Academic Vocabulary Class. Then he realizes the information sheets are not as helpful as he had hoped.

Teachers can best adapt and prepare instruction for learners that they know well, so learning about learners is time well spent. Basic information, such as most of the points that Michael included on his profile sheet, is interesting, but only somewhat helpful. Length of time studying or speaking English and test scores are more helpful in that they provide some indication of a learner's current ability. Including more information about what other languages a learner knows, how much schooling he or she has had and in what language(s), and the learner's goals (get a degree, pursue graduate studies, obtain a specific job, carry out a particular work function) is also valuable. Having this type of information will give Michael a good starting point for developing a learning plan. For example, if he sees that many of the learners are engineering majors, he might include technical words as part of a future vocabulary lesson.

Learning about adult learners' cultures and histories and getting to know their personalities helps teachers form supportive relationships, advise learners on their academic and career English learning goals, and provide instruction that is relevant and interesting to them. Teachers who familiarize themselves with different cultures can determine a lot about how well a learner might be prepared for academic, professional, or occupational work. Values, traditions, social and political relationships, shared history, geographic location, language, social class, and religion determine many aspects of personality and lay out pathways for dealing with the world (Nieto & Bode, 2011). Learners' success will be determined in part by their ability and experience in learning English, but also by their culture, history, personality, and academic and occupational goals. Figure 3.1 indicates areas for teachers to explore when getting to know a new learner.

> **FIGURE 3.1.** Important characteristics to know about English learners
>
> **What teachers need to know about their learners' education, language background, and resources**
>
> Academic goals
> Access to supportive resources
> Access to technology
> Challenges (time management, study skills, etc.)
> Cultural background
> Cultural knowledge
> Educational background
> English courses taken
> Family background
> Favorite courses
> Gifts and talents
> Hobbies and leisure activities
> Home country
> Home language
>
> Interests
> Learning preferences
> Length of time in English-speaking setting
> Level of literacy in home language
> Level of proficiency in the four English domains
>   (listening, speaking, reading, writing)
> Life experiences
> Motivations (intrinsic and extrinsic)
> Other competencies required
> Other languages spoken
> Pragmatic knowledge
> Professional/career goals
> Special needs
> Work experience (past and current, if applicable)

PRACTICE 1A Teachers gain information about their learners.

Teachers collect information about their learners' linguistic and educational backgrounds to determine the best placement and most useful lesson plans for them. They analyze the characteristics of the language and culture of the academic, professional, or occupational discourse community that the learners seek to enter, and gather input from its members (such as faculty, supervisors, and managers), to determine what achievement of learners' goals will entail. They also develop an awareness of the learners' cultural and geographic backgrounds as a resource for planning and advising.

Examples of Practice 1a

Teachers conduct intake protocols. Many ESP programs have developed protocols to assist teachers in collecting the basic information outlined in Figure 3.1. Some of the information may be provided directly by the learners themselves, as in the example of Michael Williams above. Other information may come from the university, PLI, or IEP admissions process or from the corporate human resources department. The information collected through an intake protocol is related to the type of program. For example, EAP programs may use standardized test scores, other types of placement or diagnostic testing, learner transcripts, and learner application materials, whereas EPP and EOP programs may use oral proficiency interviews, task-based assessments, and employee biographies or records. In all cases, however, the goal is to develop an understanding of the English courses that will benefit learners as they prepare for degree coursework, prepare for a career beyond academia, or develop their language skills as they proceed through their working lives. The data gathered on such protocols is important, but it should be seen as only a starting point for further investigation.

Teachers collect and/or review linguistic and cultural background information from the cultures represented in their courses and programs. Teachers can collect data on the learners prior to the start of a course in some cases, or from the learners themselves at its beginning. In a workplace context this might be before the course design process even starts. Teachers can also gather data on the demographics at the institution or workplace and plan accordingly. Read literature on the given populations, especially if there is a large number of learners from a new culture or language group.

Teachers can be pre-emptive! It is helpful to gather this information when getting to know learners during class time or by using profile sheets that learners complete on the first day of class, near the beginning of the term, or when they join the class. Knowing this information may help teachers identify strengths and weaknesses that learners have in acquiring English language skills and academic or professional competences. Staying abreast of literature and research can also help with planning. For example, the literature on intercultural communication can guide teachers' understanding of learning challenges for adult learners from different language backgrounds, perceptions learners may have of peer feedback, and ideas learners may have about plagiarism.

Teachers or programs conduct a needs assessment. As mentioned in Chapter 1, needs assessment is a fundamental practice in ESP. In professional and occupational contexts, collecting background on the learners might be a small part of the needs analysis. The other part will be determining the type of language that learners will need for their professional goals. This work will typically involve consulting with stakeholders to determine the learning objectives prior to even meeting the learners, as well as meeting expert insiders who are already competent in the target language, are familiar with the target situations, and can give very specific advice about what is actually required.

In EAP contexts, where similar courses are run year after year, needs assessment takes place when a course is initially designed, for example through interviews with graduates about their experiences after graduation and with employers about employability. A similar needs assessment process may take place when courses are reviewed for revision and updating. However, in relation to individual learners, needs assessment is mainly related to placement decisions, as a way to decide which course is most appropriate for a given learner. For this purpose, programs can use a standardized assessment or a placement test developed for their program. Examples of standardized and commercial assessments to identify learner needs include

- Test of English as a Foreign Language (TOEFL)®
- Accuplacer®
- International English Language Testing System (IELTS)™
- Speaking Proficiency English Assessment Kit (SPEAK)®
- COMPASS® (for ESL)
- Michigan English Placement Test by CaMLA

Programs may also opt to create their own tests as an additional or alternative source of placement information. Most of such tests have a listening, speaking, and writing component. Others may include grammar, reading, or vocabulary. Program-developed tests are common in ESP settings to target the tasks and skills needed by the learners.

Teachers organize and share information about learners. The information collected through needs assessment should be available to all of the program's teachers. Some programs have a shared database that all teachers can access. It is important to provide common guidelines for sharing information, especially since learners will move through different levels, which are taught by different teachers.

PRACTICE 1B Teachers embrace and leverage the resources that learners bring to the classroom to enhance learning.

Teachers tap their learners' prior knowledge purposefully in their teaching. They try to determine what talents and work experience learners bring to the classroom, what interests and disciplines or majors motivate them, what life experiences they have had that are curriculum-related, and what else in their backgrounds has influenced their personalities and beliefs. For example, teachers can find out what computer or online experience and skills learners have already, as well as what occupational or work skills learners have or need. Knowing such information can inform content and course objectives.

Examples of Practice 1b

Teachers create forms and/or schedule individual meetings, office hours, or informal opportunities to get to know their learners. Engaging in one-on-one meetings with learners to gain knowledge about their experiences and concerns is helpful in putting them at ease. Talking with learners and asking them questions before, during, or after class may be intimidating, especially if they are new to the country, the workplace, or the program.

Teachers act as cultural mediators for learners. Providing opportunities for learners to discuss differences or conflicts among cultures and analyze the variations between the mainstream culture and other cultural systems enables them to learn about and honor other cultures and clarify their own identities. This helps learners develop positive cross-cultural relationships and teaches to avoid perpetuating prejudice, stereotyping, and racism. The goal is to create a learning environment in the classroom that encourages diverse learners to celebrate and affirm one another, work collaboratively for mutual success, and dispel powerlessness and oppression (Gay, 2010). Note that the word "culture" means much more than national culture. In ESP contexts, many other perspectives may be relevant, including workplace culture, professional culture, learning culture, and so on. (See other resources for advocacy at http://www.tesol.org/advance-the-field/advocacy-resources.)

Teachers draw on learners' native languages and cultures to build rich understandings. Teachers can connect content learning with learners' current and prior understandings and native languages. For example, the use of translations to learn vocabulary should not be discouraged (Folse, 2004). If learners keep vocabulary logs, teachers can encourage them to write translations in their native language in addition to writing a definition in English. Other examples might be identifying native language cognates in a science passage in a reading course, allowing learners to write translations or notes when teaching note-taking in a listening course, or saying a cognate or word in their native language or asking a classmate with the same native language how to say something in English in a speaking class.

Principle 2. Create Conditions for Language Learning

Gabriela Jiménez teaches an oral presentation class in an EAP program in which all the learners are matriculated into the university but are pursuing a variety of different majors. They will have to give presentations in their required courses. The learners have similar language proficiency levels but are relatively inexperienced when talking in front of an audience. Gabriela has decided to make the first speech assignment an "old bag" or "any old bag will do" speech. She has selected this speech to ease the learners' nervousness, build their confidence, and create a community. This is accomplished because the learners choose three items, one each from the past, present, and future, that they would place in the bag, and the bag itself symbolizes something about the learner's life. The learners respond positively. They appreciate being able to talk about familiar content and they enjoy learning about each other, which will make presenting easier as the course progresses.

English learners come from a variety of countries, speak many different languages, and may or may not be nervous about leaving contexts where their English language classes were filled with peers who spoke the same language, allowing the comfort of using the native language when needed. They may have left their friends and family members to study in the United States or another English-speaking country, or they may find themselves in a professional or occupational setting where English is the common language. Alternatively, they may be in courses in their countries of origin but be new to learning academic or specialized English. Teachers respond to these very understandable anxieties by creating a classroom culture that will ensure that all learners feel confident and welcome in the class.

PRACTICE 2A **Teachers promote a supportive learning environment, with attention to reducing learners' anxiety and developing trust.**

Teachers apply their knowledge of the positive conditions that promote language learning as they make decisions regarding the physical environment and the social integration of learners based on gender or cultural norms, age, English level, or other factors. They then begin to plan for instruction that will engage learners and ensure their success within and beyond the English classroom. Within an EOP or EPP context this may include finding ways to deal with learners who may be from quite different levels in the company hierarchy, or who have quite different educational backgrounds. Consider, for example, a business English class which contains a senior manager and a secretary, or an English for medical purposes class which contains a mixture of doctors, nurses, and administrative staff. Tensions can easily arise, especially when the senior manager or the "better educated" person is less competent in English.

Examples of Practice 2a

Teachers ensure that learners feel welcome and at ease. They show respect for the learners and promote community. The following activities may be useful in your class to give learners opportunities to get to know each other:

- **Find Someone Who**: Learners are given a survey sheet with characteristics such as "has one sibling" or "works late at night." They move around the room in an effort to find someone who fits each of those characteristics.
- **Year of the Coin**: Learners are each given a penny and must look at the year their coin was made and then tell the rest of the group what they were doing in that year. It can be something significant or insignificant.
- **Name Game**: There are many versions of the Name Game. One of the most common is everyone saying their name and something they like to do.

There are many books available which give examples of such classroom activities (e.g., Chan & Frendo, 2014; Harding, 2007; Master & Brinton, 1997), and teachers are well advised to consult these from time to time.

Teachers put an advance organizer on the board. An advance organizer is a tool to help both teachers and learners manage the wealth of information typically covered in the classroom. This tool helps learners understand and remember content. It is used at the beginning of class to introduce the topic and connect it to previously learned content. A simple advance organizer is a lesson agenda posted on the board that teachers can refer back to as different parts of the lesson are covered. Graphic organizers are another type of advance organizer. One type of graphic organizer is a three-column K-W-L chart. In the first column, after the topic is introduced but before the main lesson begins, learners write what they think they know about the topic. At the same time, or perhaps after a brief introduction, learners complete the second column, writing what they want to know about the topic. At the end of the lesson, learners complete the third column with what they have learned. See Figure 3.1.

FIGURE 3.1 K-W-L chart

TOPIC: _____

What I KNOW	What I WANT to know	What I LEARNED

Teachers use an LMS (Learning Management System) or CMS (Course Management System). Teachers list course and lesson objectives, post announcements, post course materials, host discussions, list assignments, collect assignments, give quizzes, and maintain grades, among other things, on an online LMS or CMS. Learners have access to the management system 24 hours a day, making it easier for both learners and teachers to implement and manage learning. There are several open-source management systems that are commonly used at a myriad of programs, including Moodle, Blackboard, and Canvas. Management systems that vary in price and licensing options include Schoology, Edmodo, Quizlet, and Google Classroom. Many of these systems and options have applications that learners can access on handheld devices such as phones or tablets. Many universities and PLIs have programs, license agreements, or access already. Other organizations, such as large multinationals, may already have their own in-house systems in place.

Teachers design appropriate physical classroom learning space. Many university classrooms and corporate training spaces have moveable furniture. When possible, teaches should arrange the furniture based on the lesson or course objectives to ensure that learners will be able to interact, ask for help, or work collaboratively. Even when teaching in a shared classroom or training room, if they can teachers should use wall space to display relevant materials or to communicate content information, as well as using the blackboard, whiteboards, or projection system (e.g., smart board).

Teachers prepare syllabuses or other information to help learners understand the objectives and expectations of the course. A syllabus or course information sheet is a contract of sorts between the teacher and the learners. It helps the teacher prepare and organize the course; it helps the learners have a clear idea of the content and what they are expected to do and learn. Common items on a syllabus include course description, assignments, assessments, policies, expectations, course objectives, and contact information for the teacher.

Some syllabi include a detailed schedule of topics, chapters, or readings for each course meeting. There might even be information explaining and modeling feedback techniques that will be used. It is common for the syllabus to be prepared in advance by the teacher or the course organizer, but in some ESP contexts it may be much more appropriate to discuss the syllabus with the learners before it is finalized. Such a syllabus, sometimes described as a "negotiated" syllabus, ensures that the learners actively participate in the course design, effectively inputting their own thoughts, ideas, and learning goals into what happens. A negotiated syllabus, especially when combined with similarly constructed rubrics and other evaluation procedures, can go far in increasing motivation and commitment (Nation & Macalister, 2010).

Teachers arrange or identify peer, tutor, or mentor opportunities. Mentoring helps learners develop their English outside the classroom, meet other people, and use other campus or school resources. A mentor can help the learner understand the language, the culture, and/or the program. Teacher can recommend mentors or mentoring opportunities to learners or arrange their own mentoring programming, such as conversation partners, cultural programs, tutoring and writing centers, and clubs or other organizations.

Teachers use clear, patterned, and routine language, assignments, examples, and models to communicate with learners. Using patterned speech and language learning routines can be helpful, particularly with learners with lower levels of language proficiency. Clarity includes providing both oral and written directions with every assignment, including step-by-step instructions, and breaking larger projects down into milestone assignments to ease learners' concerns about their ability to complete. For example, a research paper can have several milestones, such as proposal, sources, introduction, rough draft, with their own deadlines before the final paper is due; a similar approach can be used for preparing a business or professional presentation. Teachers can also include samples of previous learners' work or models of what they expect learners to produce.

PRACTICE 2B Teachers demonstrate expectations of success for all learners.

Achievement is affected by teacher expectations of success both in the English course and beyond, whether that be in academic courses, degree programs, or professional careers. A teacher with high expectations will exhibit positive behaviors toward learners, motivating them to perform at high levels. This will serve learners well beyond the English course because professors in mainstream courses and learners' eventual colleagues and bosses will expect them to perform regardless of their native language. Learners will eventually be in settings where English must be used and not everyone has the same experience an English teacher has in listening to and understanding non-native speakers of the language. It is beneficial to prepare learners to interact with native speakers who expect them to communicate as well as others in English and may not know the learner's native language. By holding high expectations, communicating them clearly to all learners regardless of native language, language proficiency, or goals, and demonstrating the belief that each learner can meet those expectations, teachers in ESP courses give their learners confidence in their ability to meet and manage such situations.

Examples of Practice 2b

Teachers demonstrate the belief that all learners in the classroom will achieve learning objectives and outcomes. Teachers state expectations clearly and consider in advance how they will scaffold learning to ensure that all learners are engaged and successful (see Practice 3b for more information on scaffolding). They remind learners that the teacher is there to help them with the content. They provide descriptive rubrics and assessment information that is transparent, identifies the different levels of performance, and uses positive terminology such as "exceeding expectations," "meeting expectations," and "approaching expectations" with short and precise descriptors. They introduce the rubrics with each assignment so that learners know exactly what is being evaluated. They explain how, when, and why rubrics are used and make sure items are clear so learners know what is expected (see Practice 5c for more information on classroom assessments). They reiterate expectations and objectives throughout the term.

Teachers praise and critique learners appropriately in order to communicate how success is achieved. Hyland (2004) states that in academic writing, such as book reviews, praise is often global but criticism is specific. This idea can be applied to learner feedback as well. Teachers should praise learners for effort, persistence, and organization just as often as they offer critique. They should be specific with feedback. For example, when evaluating learner writing, comments such as *Unclear* or *Wrong verb tense* do not communicate exactly what the learner needs to do differently. A more specific and helpful comment would be, *Your organization of the essay was good* (global), *but the verb tenses alternate between past and present, so it is hard for a reader to understand which things were true before and which things are true now* (specific). Feedback of this sort will encourage the learner to replicate the organization while seeing exactly what needs to be corrected. Feedback should be directive for learners to improve performance, and it should avoid ambiguity like *nice job* or *needs improvement*. Teacher language that values risk-taking and effort promotes a growth mindset (Dweck, 2006), as in these examples: *You got better because you wrote several drafts; You thought carefully about which verb tenses to use; Your effort is paying off; You figured out the best sentence frames to use to convey your ideas.*

Teachers use a wide variety of instructional approaches to appeal to diverse learners. When teachers create conditions for learning, they consider learner preferences and best practices based on second language acquisition research. Teachers may need to improvise based on the facility, technology, and equipment available. This means that at times teachers may choose small-group or individualized learning. They may break down complex content and tasks into incremental, step-by-step processes. They may use alternative formats, such as computers, video, demonstrations, and role-playing. They may augment learning with art or music or engage in cooperative learning projects. These choices depend on the needs and interests of the learners. For example, flipped learning allows English learners to study material at their own pace outside of class and permits the instructor to differentiate instruction for individual learners in class (Brinks Lockwood, 2014). Project-based instruction engages learners in a project over an extended period of time during which they study a real-world problem or try to answer a complex question (Buck Institute for Education, 2018 see also brief introduction in Chapter 1). Community-engaged learning integrates course learning objectives with the community off campus or outside of the program. These approaches also prepare learners by building tasks that are specifically related to professional workplaces and mainstream classes where these projects and learning frameworks are frequently used.

Teachers teach learners strategies to increase their abilities to participate in academic, professional, and occupational contexts beyond the course. The goals of learners in ESP courses focus on being able to use English effectively in their academic and professional careers, so these learners need to develop skills and strategies for reading, writing, listening, and speaking that they can use in those contexts. One effective technique is to ask learners to model a typical interaction such as a business meeting or an academic discussion. Assign groups carefully with alternating leaders facilitating the discussions and content. Teachers can list key words and phrases that learners will encounter and be expected to use in these interactions. They can also provide sentence frames that will help learners recognize common language that they will hear and know how to respond appropriately. For example, when asking learners to model a meeting on how to address a problem, a teacher might write *I think/feel/consider . . .* , *In my opinion, . . .* *To me . . .* , *To my mind . . .* , and *It goes without saying that . . .* on the board and encourage learners to use and listen for those during the conversation. Teachers should also remember to ask learners to process and discuss new content several times. By posing frequent questions and requiring learners to answer or participate in activities, teachers help learners understand new content, practice English skills, and become able to apply them in their future positions.

PRACTICE 2C Teachers plan instruction to enhance and support learners' motivation for language learning.

The study of English for academic, professional, and occupational purposes can be difficult and time consuming, and learners may not see the benefits of spending time and energy in classes if the content is not specifically geared to supporting their future goals. However, as the research discussed in Chapter 2 makes clear, motivation is an important condition for language learning. Teachers therefore need to work to engage their learners by planning lessons that are useful and relevant to their academic and professional objectives and motivate them to work persistently at learning the English they need to succeed.

Examples of Practice 2c

Teachers prompt learners to make connections from their learning to their own lives and experiences. Connections with English learners' lives help them feel a part of the learning experience and internalize their understanding of the content. They might make connections to self, world, work, or other readings and content. For example, a reading teacher in an EAP program may have learners practice skimming and scanning on a biology textbook chapter so they can connect this skill to their plans for taking university classes in microbiology. Similarly, a teacher in an aviation English course may have learners review the typical structure of air traffic control communications and then practice listening to live ones.

Teachers build a repertoire of learning tasks that learners enjoy and experience as inherently motivating. Teachers continually add new teaching ideas to their knowledge base and select from them strategically to inspire their learners. Some examples include gamification, flipped learning, role plays, situational simulations, experiential activities, storytelling, experiments, music, corpus-based research, computer-based research, and music or songs. In EAP contexts, the textbook and its ancillaries may provide websites, online programs, or expansion ideas; in EOP and EPP situations, these can sometimes be identified through the stakeholder input that is collected during the needs assessment. Bear in mind that teachers will sometimes have to develop their own materials in order to ensure alignment with learning objectives. Offer extra credit or a list of resources and websites for learners to get additional practice with pronunciation, vocabulary, or grammar. When learners have a choice in participating and choosing activities, they are often more involved and motivated.

Teachers help learners focus on a well-defined project with a future outcome to motivate and structure their behavior. Project-based learning is an ideal way to accomplish this practice. It improves classroom dynamics by engaging learners in a group project with a learner-selected topic or questions and a well-defined outcome. Teachers have flexibility regarding the length of a project, which may last from one or two weeks in a business English course to an entire 16-week semester in an IEP. Learners take ownership of their work and appreciate the challenges of solving a complex problem. While teachers can choose the topics, better results may occur if learners select the project focus themselves, connecting it to their own lives, their future major or profession, or their personal interests. For instance, a group involved in environmental studies might prepare a project about saving the campus's trees. Those interested in becoming medical professionals might develop a plan for making treatment for a specific disease available and accessible to people of limited means.

Teachers expect learner ownership and support learners in engagement with learning. When learners are actively engaged, they process concepts more deeply. They are open to thinking out loud, venturing opinions, seeking clarification and comprehension, participating in discussions, questioning and evaluating ideas, and interpreting and drawing conclusions. Teachers can promote learner ownership by using methods such as flipped learning, project-based learning, and community-engaged learning. Ownership can also be established by offering opportunities for peer-to-peer interaction and learner choice and by using material relevant to learners' future goals, such as explaining a section of a physics textbook or describing the architecture of a well-known building. When learners themselves are involved in making decisions about what and how they learn, the result is a negotiated syllabus, which was introduced in Practice 2a and which is an excellent way to increase learner ownership.

Principle 3. Design High-Quality Lessons for Language Development

Paige Fillion is teaching a listening and speaking skills course that prepares learners to engage in oral business interactions. The course uses an ESP textbook, and one chapter includes a short business talk on marketing a new product. Paige first plays the talk and tests learners' listening comprehension by asking main idea and detail questions. Once she confirms that the learners comprehend the content, she asks them to look at existing marketing for products and places they are familiar with and has them analyze how the content from the lecture is being applied to these authentic examples. Finally, she puts the learners into groups and asks them to create a new product and write a marketing campaign. Learners present their products and campaigns to the other groups at the end of the lesson.

Effective teachers design lessons that promote the development of learning and thinking strategies. Careful planning can support the application of Bloom's taxonomy when learners are learning a new language and new content. Bloom's taxonomy (Anderson & Krathwohl, 2001; Bloom et al., 1956) was created to encourage higher-order thinking skills that move learners beyond knowledge and comprehension into application, analysis, evaluation, and synthesis. When teachers design lessons using Bloom's taxonomy, learners move beyond simple remembering (memorizing) and understanding (basic comprehension) to applying learning and thinking strategies that build language proficiency, content knowledge, and ability to use the acquired language and knowledge to accomplish specific tasks or objectives.

PRACTICE 3A Teachers prepare lessons with clear outcomes and convey them to their learners.

Teachers can guide learners to a lesson's essential language learning and content learning objectives more efficiently when both teachers and learners are aware of the important outcomes of the learning experience. In all ESP contexts, those outcomes are defined by the ways in which learners are able to use their knowledge of language and content in service to specific purposes—in other words, performance objectives. The performance objective may be to compare two position papers and write a summary report, to participate in a presentation or debate, or to train new employees in the use of a piece of equipment, for example.

When setting objectives, specificity and communication are key (Short & Echevarría, 2016). It is useful for all teachers to have language, content, and performance objectives in each lesson and for the class as a whole to know what those objectives are. Learning strategy objectives are also beneficial. The objectives for each lesson should be connected overtly to the overall objectives for the course and to learners' academic, professional, or occupational needs and goals, so that learners understand what they are expected to learn and why.

In addition to using Bloom's taxonomy, teachers can remember the mnemonic acronym SMART, introduced by Doran (1981) to emphasize the importance of objectives and the challenges in setting them. The SMART mnemonic has been used extensively in both the business world and teacher lesson planning. One common explanation of the acronym is the following:

S = Specific
M = Measurable
A = Attainable
R = Realistic
T = Time-related

Examples of Practice 3a

Teachers develop language and content objectives aligned to learning outcomes. Consider the following when planning for overall course content and individual lessons before a course begins:

- To determine content objectives, ask these questions:

    S: *What specifically do I want or need my learners to be able to know or do with the content by the end of class? How can I communicate the objective to the learners?*

    M: *Can achievement of my objective be measured? How?*

    A: *Is my objective level-appropriate? Is it cognitively challenging? What contextual supports can I provide?*

    R: *How does my objective help learners achieve their goal of [entering the university, becoming a nurse]?*

    T: *Can my objective be achieved within the time I have allotted to it?*

- To determine language objectives, ask these questions:

    S: *What specifically do I want my learners to understand, say, read, or write by the end of class?*

    M: *Can achievement of my objectives be measured? How?*

    A: *What specific language structures and vocabulary are necessary to convey the content? What grammatical forms do I want my learners to use and understand? What language functions do my learners need to use to accomplish success in this lesson? What contextual supports can I provide for learning?*

    R: *How will the language skills I teach help learners to be successful academically or professionally? How can I communicate how these skills transfer to academic or professional settings?*

    T: *Can my objectives be achieved within the time I have allotted to them?*

- To determine learning strategy objectives, ask these questions:

    S: *What specific learning strategy will I teach or demonstrate to help my learners learn more efficiently? How can I communicate my objective to my learners?*

    M: *Can achievement of my objective be measured? How?*

    A: *What learning strategy will I use to help my learners be better prepared for their future academic studies or work in professional/occupational contexts?*

    R: *What learning strategies will help my learners succeed in their target academic, occupational, or professional settings? Is my objective appropriate for my learners?*

    T: *Can my objective be achieved within the time I have allotted for it (Levine & McCloskey, 2013)?*

Sample Language and Content Objectives in an Academic Setting

	Language objective	Content objective
Reading	Learners will read and annotate a college textbook chapter.	Learners will summarize a textbook chapter.
Writing	Learners will write the introduction to a research report using common introductory frames.	Learners will conduct research on a banking topic and list relevant information.
Listening	Learners will identify key words that indicate importance, examples, facts, and opinions in speech.	Learners will listen to a university lecture excerpt and record main points in their notes.
Speaking	Learners will make statements using phrases to express opinions, agreement, and disagreement.	Learners will participate in a panel discussion or debate about a current event.
Grammar	Learners will use if-then and other conditional phrases in speaking.	Learners will identify causes and effects related to a mock trial court case.
Vocabulary	Learners will define political science vocabulary terms.	Learners will read a political science news article or passage with new vocabulary terms.

Teachers develop the course syllabus and individual lessons with step-by-step achievement of learning objectives in mind. Learners need to see that they are developing the skills and knowledge that they will need when they move on to their target professional, occupational, or academic contexts. Each lesson therefore needs to end with learners actually using their new language skills and content knowledge in a task or activity that simulates real communication situations as closely as possible—that is, with an activity that shows learners they have achieved the performance objective(s). However, learners also need considerable support in developing new knowledge and trying it out in a non-threatening environment where they are comfortable making mistakes and receiving feedback before they apply it in a more exposed context.

Instructors can ensure that they provide such support for their ESP learners by designing lessons using a three part presentation—guided practice—communicative practice sequence. For example, in an EOP lesson for airline personnel where the objective is to be able to explain options for changing an airline reservation to a customer, the teacher would open the lesson with a brief explanation of the lesson objective followed by a presentation of typical requests, questions, and needs that the customer might express and appropriate ways of responding to them. The teacher would both model the language and elicit examples from learners of relevant conversations they have heard or experienced. Then learners would engage in structured practice, which might include completing a cloze worksheet that contains a short example conversation with blanks where key vocabulary should be filled in, or drawing customer statements/questions on sentence strips from a hat and then providing an answer, or using the sentence strips Jeopardy-style, drawing the answers and having to provide the customer question or statement. From this the lesson could move to having learners work in pairs to develop the script for a role play in which one of them is the customer and the other is the airline representative.

Teachers communicate course objectives to learners. Telling learners once about the overall course objectives may not be enough, and learners may need to be reminded several times throughout the course. In addition to listing course objectives on the syllabus or course information sheet, prominently display course objectives on course websites and course management systems. Also explain the objectives of specific lessons or course content at the beginning of each class or book chapter. Use phrases such as *Today, we're going to . . .* , *This will help you . . .* , *By the end of this class, you should be able to . . .* , *This is important for [when you enter mainstream classes] . . .* For assignments and projects, show exemplars (e.g. sample essays, a correctly annotated reading, good notes from a listening class, a video of a group discussion) of the eventual outcome of a content objective or series of objectives in a course.

PRACTICE 3B Teachers provide and enhance input through varied approaches, techniques, and modalities.

Comprehensible and enhanced input is necessary for communicating with language learners. To prepare to meet this need, teachers ask themselves questions regarding the implementation of the content, such as *How will the new information be conveyed to my learners? Will they listen to it, read it, or engage in research or an inquiry task to discover it? How can I support the input with context and scaffolding? How can I be sure that my learners understand my input?* Varied approaches, techniques, and modalities include flipped learning, project-based learning, design thinking, community engaged learning, lectures, discussions, and demonstrations.

Examples of Practice 3b

Teachers use comprehensible input to convey information to learners. Comprehensible input is extremely important to help learners make progress in the target language. Whether oral or written, comprehensible input helps English learners understand the meaning of the communication. Teachers scaffold language input in multiple ways to aid perception and promote understanding. Comprehensibility scaffolds, explanatory devices for increased clarity, and modeling and demonstration are among the many techniques that teachers use. These three types of scaffolds are highlighted in Table 3.1 Multiple scaffolds can be used in tandem to aid learner success.

Table 3.1 Scaffolding for comprehensibility

Scaffolding for comprehensibility	Explanatory devices for comprehensibility	Modeling and demonstrations
Nonverbal cues (gestures, facial expressions)	Visual aids (maps, charts, graphs, graphic organizers, drawings, illustrations, photos)	Flipping the classroom or lesson
Using visual aids	Video clips	Targeting and modeling the appropriate language register (academic language, word choice)
Simplifying or elaborating	Audio supports and other multimedia	
Embedding definitions and explanations		
Allowing use of home language translation	Highlighted or bolded (annotated) text	Providing demonstrations of language in use (sample learner work, sample completed projects)
Teaching and using signal words and phrases so learners understand content	Bilingual dictionaries	
	Summaries of class content	Explicitly teaching common forms used in professions
Demonstrating		

One way to ensure comprehensibility of input is to adopt an idea from flipped learning, whether or not the lesson is flipped: new information should be conveyed and practiced with the two lowest levels of Bloom's taxonomy, paying special attention to verbs used in the directions given to learners and activities (Brinks Lockwood, 2018). For example, verbs commonly associated with the "knowledge" level of Bloom's taxonomy are list, define, and identify, and verbs commonly associated with the "understand" level are indicate, explain, or describe.

Typically, but not always, EAP learners are provided with oral language input in their mainstream classes; for example, their general education classes are lecture based. Therefore, it is important for EAP teachers to make sure learners can understand and manage this type of oral input. Since these learners are typically already literate in another language, EAP teachers may want to provide both oral and written input. The dual modalities complement each other and provide further support for meaning.

Each area of ESP has particular characteristics that distinguish it. Academic programs use academic register—the register of academic texts and instruction. Professional contexts such as law, architecture, medicine, and economics have specialized vocabulary and established registers and formats for oral and written communication, as do occupational contexts such as sales and customer service. As noted in Chapter 2, each of these specialized language types is more complex and denser than social language. Academic and professional language in particular have more abstract terms, use more complex graphics and illustrations, and provide little to no scaffolding. In most mainstream classes and professional contexts, instructors and professional colleagues have not been trained as teachers of English as a new language and will not scaffold their content for the non-native English speakers in the room. Because many English learners have acquired spoken language first and/or have not practiced with authentic content, they are rarely prepared for the academic or professional register.

All ESP teachers must therefore provide multiple opportunities for learners to receive comprehensible input and exposure to the appropriate register. These can be provided in a variety of ways, such as videos or podcasts with competent speakers, teacher explanations, discussions and partnerships with competent speakers, and authentic texts.

Teachers adjust their language to enhance input to learners. When teachers enhance input, they make it more usable for learners, who may then perceive target features of the language more clearly. The enhancements used by teachers may be verbal or visual. For example, teachers may

- Speak clearly
- Speak at a normal rate
- Use varied repetition
- Use gestures as clues to meanings
- Use word stress, intonation, and/or pauses purposefully (perhaps to mimic what learners will hear outside the ESP classroom)
- Recast learner language in ways that approach the target
- Contrast forms
- Explain idioms, jargon, and slang typical of native speech
- Write down key words or include them on presentation slides
- Use signal words and phrases (and teach them)
- Elicit oral production or elaboration from learners

Teachers use multiple sources of input with learners. When teachers add visuals or audio supports to written text, they increase the comprehensibility of the material. Other sources of input include

- Movies and video
- Music
- Websites and social media
- Podcasts
- Paired talk or paired reading
- Peer mentoring
- Small-group discussion
- Course management and learning management sites
- Extra online or print activities and practice
- Presentations accompanied by visuals, outlines, notecards, and peer support

Teachers use clear instructions to direct learning tasks. Teachers use consistent classroom management practices throughout the duration of the course to help learners understand what is expected of them in the ESP classroom as well as in other academic and professional settings. Teachers should use clear directions, ideally provided both orally and in written form. Where possible, teachers should make themselves available before class, after class, or during office hours so they have an opportunity to clarify instructions.

Remember that multistep directions can be broken down into step-by-step procedures, with each step modeled or shown with exemplars as needed. For example, when teaching graduate learners how to write a journal article, teach the different sections of a research article, such as introduction, methods, results, and discussion, separately while having learners read both published models and learner models before writing their own sections. For learners to perform well, teachers must show learners *how* to do whatever it is they are being asked to do. Another useful technique is for the teacher to ask appropriate questions to check that learners have understood the instructions.

PRACTICE 3C Teachers engage learners in the use and practice of authentic language and materials.

ESP learners grow their language skills through the use of authentic interaction and materials. In ineffective ESP classrooms, learners might be mostly silent, sitting quietly while the teacher talks, and using materials that lack authentic reading or listening passages or spoken language used by native speakers. As a result, these English learners might not be exposed to the types of materials and language they need to be successful beyond the English classroom. Although authentic materials can be more challenging, they do mirror real-world tasks that learners will be asked to perform in their academic studies and workplaces. In an EFL teaching context, this is especially important since they are learning English in a non-English speaking country or setting. They need to practice with real textbook readings, lecture excerpts, and speaking activities to make them more effective. By seeing and practicing with authentic materials, learners are more likely to achieve their goals. They will need to be able to participate in classrooms and eventually work in settings where they must speak up, ask questions, and understand the responses.

Examples of Practice 3c

Teachers elicit output from learners. The four modalities (listening, speaking, reading, and writing) are interrelated processes that rely on and develop from and with one another. For example, listening to oral language and reading are receptive processes, both of which require an active and engaged mind to construct meaning from the spoken or written content. Speaking and writing are productive processes; speaking can help learners develop the ability to write in the target language, and writing (particularly of outlines and mind maps) can help them prepare for more complex speaking tasks such as presentations.

To design activities that will elicit authentic output, it may be helpful to consider ways of thinking about language skills, which were described in Chapter 2. Noting that the division into four modalities listed above does not capture "real" communication, both the Common European Framework of Reference for Languages (CEFR) and the American Council on the Teaching of Foreign Languages Proficiency Guidelines (ACTFL) describe language use in terms of the type of interaction: one way or two way. CEFR presents activities under four modes: reception (listening and reading), production (spoken and written), interaction (spoken and written), and mediation (translation and interpreting) (Council of Europe, 2018). The ACTFL Proficiency Guidelines describe language proficiency in terms of three modes: interpretive, interactive, and presentational (ACTFL, 2012; Sandrock, 2010). Both encourage teachers to identify which of these modes are relevant to their learners and have learners use the ones that they are more likely to encounter in "real life." So, for example, a teacher in an EOP course for hospitality industry staff might teach listening and speaking with a two-way focus on role plays that simulate interactions with hotel guests, while a teacher in an EAP course for learners planning to enroll in graduate courses in history might teach listening and speaking with a one-way focus on understanding academic lectures and giving short academic presentations.

In addition, learning a new language and developing proficiency in the four modalities depend on two language foundations: grammar and vocabulary. A high level of focus on grammar, word choice/vocabulary, and fluency enables learners to make the message understandable to the listener. Speaking helps learners notice a mismatch or gap between what they *want* to say and what they *can* say. To encourage learners to notice their errors and gaps in knowledge, teachers find multiple ways to elicit output from them. This elicitation might come in the form of group discussion (speaking) or written essays (writing).

Teachers create opportunities for learners to be active participants. Some people think that language is best thought of as a verb rather than a noun (Levine & McCloskey, 2013). As such, it is best learned while *doing* something with it—by being actively engaged with and applying it in meaningful practice. Possibilities for encouraging active participation include arranging desks or tables for pair or group work and assigning learners to groups purposefully. In online courses, teachers can assign learners to specific break-out groups to encourage interaction. Whether teachers are teaching in class or online, active participation is both possible and key for language development regardless of learners' levels of proficiency. Tasks can be designed to engage learners meaningfully regardless of proficiency level.

Unfortunately, much of what ESP learners have practiced before entering an EAP, EPP, or EOP program may not always be useful or productive for further language proficiency development. To support these learners in achieving a high level of English, instructors can help them make their talk accountable, meaning that they need to explain their thinking and language use with evidence—critical thinking. Not all talk sustains learning. For classroom talk to promote learning, it must be accountable: to the learning community, to accurate and appropriate knowledge, and to rigorous thinking (Michaels et al., 2013).

Teachers in all types of ESP instruction can make classroom talk and discussion productive by using sentence frames and posing questions to elicit production.

- Can you expand on that?
- So, you are saying that . . .
- Why do you agree/disagree?
- What makes you say that?/Why do you think that?
- What do you think?
- Who can add more on . . . ?

Instructors can also elicit production by establishing collaborative groups in the classroom or even outside the classroom or online using the course management system. This allows them to include all learners in the conversation, even if some learners might be quieter or less confident about their English skills during class. To ensure that discussions are productive, instructors must make sure each one has a clear goal or outcome and requires critical thinking. It can be beneficial to use materials, content, and activities related to learners' academic or professional goals. For example, an EPP or EOP class might have a discussion with simulated problem situations specific to the career field that learners plan to enter; learners would discuss what to do in each situation.

Teachers use techniques to promote active language practice in a variety of settings. Teachers can provide opportunities for learners to be involved throughout the class. Different techniques are useful at various stages of a lesson, as illustrated in the examples in Table 3.2.

Table 3.2 Language practice techniques

Language practice techniques throughout a lesson	
Starting instruction	• K-W-L (What I Know, What I Want to Know, What I Learned) • Making predictions • Pre-reading or pre-listening strategies • Discussion questions • Activating prior knowledge
Building instruction	• Group text reading • Sentence frames • Analysis (example: script analysis for speaking) • Note-taking • Reading, writing, listening, and speaking techniques
Applying instruction	• Graphic organizers • Case studies • Making connections • Situational simulations and role plays • Exercises and activities in and out of class
Concluding instruction	• Reflections (about lesson and content) • Peer review • Rubrics • Comprehension checks • Reviewing content • Summarizing

Teachers integrate language learning into content lessons and content learning into language lessons. Teaching study skills, time management, and the content topics necessary for academic or professional success is an essential part of all types of ESP instruction. An awareness of the content learners will face beyond the ESL classroom is imperative for learner success. Learners will be expected to understand content, participate in discussions and meetings, make inferences, draw conclusions, and cite examples and evidence. Content is also the vehicle for language development, so teachers with primary responsibility for language development must incorporate vocabulary, oral interaction, reading, and writing that reflect what their learners will face in their university classes or professional and occupational settings.

Each content area has specific vocabulary and syntactic structures, as well as specific genres and discourse characteristics, that may overlap with generalized knowledge of English only partially or not at all. However, some content areas share characteristics that can allow ESP instructors to develop lessons that address the needs and goals of learners who are pursuing different fields of study or professional endeavor.

Teachers encourage language learning beyond the classroom. Although some learners may live in areas where English is not routinely spoken, teachers can encourage authentic language learning and practice through homework assignments and projects that encourage learners to participate in activities outside the classroom.

Teachers can explore options with community-engaged learning projects, field trips, or volunteering opportunities, or they can flip their classroom so learners have more opportunities to work on projects in class using English. Teachers can also employ movies, television, newspapers, podcasts, radio, and websites in English for input. In addition, teachers can encourage language interaction through tasks such as interviewing members of their chosen profession, participating in social media exchanges, and practicing scripted dialogues.

PRACTICE 3D Teachers design lessons so that learners engage with relevant and meaningful content.

Learners are motivated to attend and participate in classroom discussions and activities when teachers deliver lessons that engage them in various ways, most importantly by using authentic, meaningful, and appropriate content that will directly prepare them for success in their academic and occupational pursuits. Teachers can use their learners' goals as a basis for lessons. When these goals are recognized and integrated into the classroom, learners recognize the importance, usefulness, and transferability of the content to their lives. This is a powerful form of motivation for all ESP learners.

Examples of Practice 3d

Teachers plan tasks that are relevant and useful to learners. As teachers get to know their adult English learners, they discover that these learners respond differently to tasks and that some may like, for example, group work, while others prefer individual assignments. Most learners share one characteristic—they respond to variety and creativity in lessons and activities. Relating content to their future goals will increase learners' engagement with the course work. For example, when teaching an EAP class, using chapters from the textbooks used in the courses learners will have to take makes reading instruction relevant and useful to the learners. EAP teachers can also use lectures posted online by college professors as their listening content. Similarly, when teaching persuasive language in an EPP course, including an assignment such as writing cover letters could be useful for learners applying for senior management positions. Oral skills courses might include listening to podcasts on field-specific topics and then making short presentations on the content.

Teachers select materials that reflect learners' specific interests. Adults learn best when instruction is relevant to their immediate needs and goals, so teachers should choose materials for their lessons thoughtfully. When teaching a class such as English for Law, use case studies to teach reading and writing. When teaching English for Nursing, incorporate vocabulary and content specific to the medical field. When courses are not specific to a field or job, consider using a flipped classroom approach that provides opportunities for learner choice of materials. For example, in a reading class, have learners study the definition and reasons for using a particular reading skill on their own. Then have them bring content of their own choosing to class, and use the class time for application of the reading skill.

PRACTICE 3E Teachers plan differentiated instruction according to their learners' English language proficiency levels, needs, and goals.

Differentiated instruction (DI) is an instructional model that provides multiple pathways to learning and offers differing challenges to a diverse learner population. Adult learners come to ESP instruction with widely varied language and cultural backgrounds, life experiences, levels of English proficiency, learning goals, and expectations for the learning process. To promote learner success, therefore, teachers must develop understanding through observation and interaction of the methods and techniques that will be most effective for each learner. DI requires that teachers scaffold instruction to promote learner success rather than reduce the complexity of instructional goals (Tomlinson, 2014). It also requires them to maintain flexibility in the teaching methods that they employ. For example, an EAP writing course may include some learners who have prior experience in academic-style summary writing and others who do not. Using a DI model, the teacher will provide guided practice in developing short summaries from relatively simple texts for the latter group, and more challenging, less structured tasks for the former. Similarly, in an EPP course for pilots, some learners may have had more opportunities than others to become familiar with the formats of typical air traffic communications. Using a DI model, the teacher will provide extensive guided instruction in what to listen for to the learners with less experience, and will challenge those with more experience by giving them more open-ended tasks to complete.

Examples of Practice 3e

Teachers build scaffolding into lessons for different purposes. Various forms of scaffolding help all learners succeed. Teachers structure learning in incremental steps and provide the level of assistance that each learner needs to be successful. The assistance may take the form of strategies for approaching a given communication task, road maps or guidelines that support learners in recognizing and producing particular discourse patterns, and structured practice in class before application outside of class. Especially important is incorporating all the levels of Bloom's taxonomy, as noted at the beginning of this chapter.

Teachers employ grouping patterns designed to promote peer support, engagement, and comprehensibility. Learners in all types of ESP courses will need to work in groups and on teams in their future academic or professional settings, and these groups will include native speakers of English and members of different ages, genders, religions, and cultures. Teachers can prepare learners to function effectively on teams while supporting their work in the ESP course by using pair work and small groups. Many teachers carefully choose the group makeup so learners have opportunities to participate fully and feel supported in their learning. Sometimes groups may be arranged by first language, proficiency level, or field of academic or professional interest. Other times, stronger learners may be grouped with weaker ones, or learners may choose their own groups.

Teachers (and learners) provide supplemental materials. Teachers may use texts written for English learners some of the time. These materials are generally developed with attention to the language and content challenges of the learners, and are often a good starting point. However, learners wanting to advance in university or professional settings need to transition to more authentic and challenging material in order to better bridge the gap between ESP classes and life beyond the ESP classroom. For example, in an EAP reading course, a teacher may first teach a reading strategy such as annotating a text and practicing on a one-page passage written for learners with controlled vocabulary, and then bring in a chapter from a general education textbook that is substantially longer and not adapted for the ESL learner. This allows learners to practice the same skill using the types of materials they will see when they leave the ESL classroom.

In EOP and EPP contexts it is common to supplement or even replace published materials with this sort of authentic input taken from the real world. Indeed, very often such "real world" texts may be the only relevant materials the teacher can find. For example, in a course in the hospitality industry, learners might need to be able to explain a local menu in English. The best way to bring such language into the classroom is with real menus. Likewise, in an in-company training context, real specification sheets belonging to industry products will be much more beneficial than anything published in an ESL textbook. Further, in a course for construction workers, a teacher would likely have to arrange for building plans and blueprints to be made available in order to facilitate authentic discussion, as such materials are not often found in many ESL textbooks. as the topic would not be found in an ESL textbook.

Teachers plan for appropriate challenges, depending on learners' language proficiency levels. Teachers prepare to modify the language level of oral instruction if necessary and incorporate modeling and demonstrations in their lessons to support comprehension. They aim for cognitive rigor, yet may develop a range of activities for learner practice. By knowing their learners' interests and levels, teachers can design lessons that challenge all learners to advance in their language skill development.

PRACTICE 3F Teachers promote the use of learning strategies, problem-solving, and critical thinking among learners.

English learners often learn new language and new content material at the same time. Additionally, they must be able to think critically and solve problems. However, critical thinking may not be taught in second language classrooms, in, for example, EFL secondary school settings, so English learners may struggle when entering university programs or professional settings. In these settings, learners will be asked to complete tasks such as thinking logically and strategically, analyzing, assessing problems, comparing elements, synthesizing information from multiple sources, applying information, formulating their own opinions, making inferences, and drawing conclusions. They need to ask questions, evaluate statements, and support or argue against points they encounter in papers, discussions, and meetings. Essentially, learners need learning strategies and practice with higher-order thinking skills, the highest levels of Bloom's taxonomy.

Examples of Practice 3f

Teachers teach a variety of learning strategies for specific purposes. Over time, teachers introduce learners to a range of learning strategies that they can apply as needed when they are trying to figure out meaning, complete an assignment, or review material. Different types of strategies have different uses and purposes.

- *Metacognitive strategies* enable learners to plan for a task, monitor their work, and evaluate effectiveness when the task is complete. Such strategies allow the learner to self-regulate and manage time, and they have broad generic applications that learners will need after leaving ESP instruction and entering the workplace or academic courses. Examples of these strategies include advance organization, organizational planning, selective attention, self-management, monitoring of comprehension, monitoring of production, and self-assessment (Chamot, 2009).

- *Cognitive strategies* involve critical thinking and are often related to specific types of tasks. For example, note taking is helpful when listening to oral language input, and word grouping is useful for vocabulary learning. Other examples of these strategies include activating prior knowledge, summarizing, creating images, reasoning by deduction/induction, using auditory representation, and highlighting text (Chamot, 2009).

- *Social/affective strategies* are important for English learners because effective academic learning and professional success involve cooperation with others and the ability to ask questions for clarification. These strategies also ease the anxiety that accompanies being a second language speaker in a dominant language group. Examples of these strategies include clarifying, asking for more information, paraphrasing, listening actively, and summarizing.

- *Language learning strategies* help learners learn the new language on their own. Examples include literacy strategies such as previewing and setting a purpose for reading and analyzing and following models for writing; skills strategies, such as the SQ3R (survey, question, read, recite, review) reading strategy; and study strategies such as flash cards, rehearsal, or vocabulary logs.

Teachers design tasks for learners to practice using critical thinking and learning strategies. Teachers need to deliberately plan challenging questions, problem-solving activities, and project tasks. Assigning activities and exercises using verbs associated with the highest levels of Bloom's taxonomy and employing flipped learning that "flips" Bloom's taxonomy allows for more higher order thinking skills to be included in lesson plans (Brinks Lockwood, 2018). Lists of common verbs associated with Bloom's taxonomy are available online.

> For a good list of verbs that demonstrate critical thinking and sample question stems, see https://www.utica.edu/academic/Asessment/new/Blooms%20Taxonomy%20-%20Best.pdf. This list can help teachers determine what learners are being asked to do.

PRACTICE 3G Teachers promote self-directed learning.

As learners move beyond English programs and into university courses or professional careers, they need to be autonomous and in control of their own learning and behaviors, including setting their own learning goals and monitoring their progress. They need to be able to manage their time and study in academic settings and their time and tasks in professional settings. This means that they need to self-regulate.

Self-directed learning involves three skills: forethought, performance, and self-assessment. Forethought involves setting goals and benchmarks for progress and employing critical thinking about effective ways of achieving learning goals. During performance, learners exercise self-control and use self-observation to monitor progress and adjust behavior as needed. In self-assessment, learners evaluate their performance and regulate their reactions. Self-regulated learners are in control of their learning outcomes (Zimmerman & Schunk, 2012). Instructors can help their learners develop a self-directed learning orientation by sequencing learning tasks in steps and providing supports such as checklists that give learners graphic representations of progress toward task completion. They can also encourage learners to form study groups and to seek out campus resources such as tutoring services and writing centers, or professional resources such as time management and project management training.

Examples of Practice 3g

Teachers facilitate learners' setting of meaningful goals for themselves and monitoring of their progress toward those goals. Many teachers accomplish learner goal setting through developing course objectives, and then having individual meetings with learners during office hours or other available times. This is part of the ongoing needs analysis which was mentioned in Chapter 1. When possible, such meetings can occur on a regular schedule. During each one-on-one meeting, the instructor and the learner can review evidence of learner accomplishments in relation to the set objectives and then identify possible goals for future progress. The instructor may then encourage the learner to make specific choices about how to achieve the goals. This process also gives the instructor time to become familiar with each learner's long-term goals so that course content and activities can be tailored to goal achievement.

Teachers provide assessment tools that allow learners to evaluate their strengths and weaknesses (and can be used to self-assess). For ESP learners, rubrics and comments on assignments help to evaluate performance in a variety of areas on a scale, such as a 1 to 5 scale. Rubrics are useful for learners at all language proficiency levels. They help learners self-evaluate by providing a set of specific criteria tied to the course objectives that will be used to evaluate performance on tasks and assignments. Various performance levels are modeled or described, using a scoring scale with numbers, letters, or other descriptive labels. When teachers clearly explain rubrics or grading criteria using language that learners comprehend, learners gain a clear understanding of what they are to know or be able to do at the end of the task. Learners can also use task rubrics themselves for self-evaluation of their performance or to provide feedback to their peers. Sometimes the criteria have been developed for previous courses and can be re-used; in other situations, particularly in EOP and EPP settings, they will need to be developed in collaboration with the relevant stakeholders.

Teachers help learners develop effective work management habits. Once learners leave the familiar ESP classroom setting, they will need to be able to manage time and study or work tasks on their own. Adult English learners thus need to develop effective study and work habits that will serve them in their future academic, professional, or occupational pursuits. Many learners do not know which habits are best, and they may find that habits that worked well for them in their native language context do not work as well in English settings, such as quantity versus quality (writing longer essays to fulfill a word count rather than writing a shorter essay that uses academic writing conventions and tone, for example). Teachers can identify effective work management strategies in all types of ESP instruction and at all language proficiency levels and integrate these into the course. Modeling and practice over time will ensure that learners have learned the strategies and can apply them.

Some productive study habits include
- Structured note-taking in lectures or presentations and meetings
- Use of graphic organizers
- Before, during, and after reading strategies
- Before, during, and after listening strategies
- Rehearsing oral presentations

Useful time management tools include
- Calendars and schedulers
- Color coding
- "To do" lists
- Priority ranking

Principle 4. Adapt Lesson Delivery as Needed

Lee Bunting teaches a listening/speaking course designed to prepare learners for college-level studies. In class, he played a listening passage for learners and saw that the learners didn't understand. He played the passage again. As a result, more learners understood, but Lee was not able to finish anything other than the main idea and detailed questions that followed the listening. He simply did not anticipate the content of the listening being so challenging for learners. He decided to flip the next lesson, so learners listened to the passage and completed the comprehension activities outside of class. In class, he was then able to move learners through the other activities and complete all the material in the course textbook.

Lee wisely decided to flip the structure of his listening/speaking lesson. Doing so allows the learners to listen to the material as many or as few times as they need to understand the content. Then, when they come to class, everyone is ready to complete the activities. This decision also allows Lee's learners to complete the easier, lower-order thinking skill activities, such as answering main idea and detail questions, on their own. In class, he is then able not only to finish all the material he planned, but also to propel learners to higher-order thinking skill activities, better preparing them for their personal academic or professional goals, while he is in the classroom to serve as a mentor.

Interactions in the classroom give teachers a great deal of information about how well learners are understanding the content, using critical thinking skills, and preparing for success outside the ESP classroom. By serving as a mentor in the classroom rather than only delivering content, an instructor can observe and reflect on learners' responses and readily see to what degree the learners are meeting the learning objectives and the learners' own goals. Often objectives are not met because of a variety of obstacles: the learners' lack of prior knowledge, the teacher's incorrect assumptions about lesson delivery, substantial differences in the learners' language proficiency levels, pacing problems, and more. If learners are not succeeding, teachers need to reflect on the causes and make adjustments to their instruction. Similarly, if lesson tasks are too easy, the teacher will want to increase the challenge. This decision making may occur frequently on any given day, and decisions sometimes need to be made in a matter of seconds.

PRACTICE 4A **Teachers check learner comprehension frequently and adjust instruction according to learner responses.**

To teach effectively, instructors need to evaluate what learners do and do not know in real time. Formative assessment, which takes place as instruction is occurring through comprehension checks, teacher observations, and learner self-evaluation, averts situations in which the instructor does not discover until the end of a lesson or unit that some learners have misunderstood a key concept or have incorrectly learned critical vocabulary.

Examples of Practice 4a

Teachers use teaching practices that ensure better auditory comprehension. Teachers need to check comprehension often throughout a class. Adult learners learn best when they are not required to sustain extended periods of concentration while simultaneously attempting to comprehend auditory input. Lessons that include extended listening tasks are more effective when the quality of the audio is high so that the sound is clear (unless the purpose of the activity is to practice understanding challenging audio, such as train station announcements or air traffic control communications). In addition, comprehension in listening activities is enhanced when learners have opportunities to interact with others about the input. Therefore, one way for instructors to make sure learners understand is to have learners talk to each other about the content of the listening passage.

Teachers check comprehension with group response techniques. Teachers can use quick comprehension checks during a lesson to gauge how the class is doing. Some group response activities include holding up response cards or collecting exit tickets or reflections at the end of class. Technology options such as Poll Everywhere that have learners use handheld devices to submit responses are especially useful in large classes and in preparing EAP learners for mainstream university classes where these group response techniques are frequently used.

PRACTICE 4B Teachers adjust their talk, the task, or the materials according to learner responses.

As a lesson unfolds, if teachers notice some confusion or misunderstanding, they make adjustments so that all learners can meet the learning goals. Teachers may vary their oral language input to ease the comprehension load. They may help learners gain access to content through the use of other forms of input, such as videos, translations, alternative texts, visual aids, and peer support. They might also adapt a task midstream, by adding more time, providing supplemental resources, or pulling a small group of learners together for reteaching while the rest of the class works independently. Flipped learning methods also allow for greater adjustments and differentiated instruction.

Examples of Practice 4b

Teachers modify their oral language input as necessary to advance comprehension and scaffold language learning. Examples of teacher adjustments include the following:

- *Simplification.* The teacher makes sentences shorter and grammatically less complex, eliminates idioms and slang, and uses fewer pronouns in extended talk. The teacher might pre-teach vocabulary in a reading or listening passage or use scripted examples in textbooks before moving to more authentic materials.
- *Wait time.* The teacher waits to allow learners time to respond to a question. The amount of time depends on the type of question asked and the level of the learners. Recall questions may require about three seconds, but higher-order thinking questions could merit a wait time of seven to ten seconds.
- *Open-ended questioning.* The teacher asks questions that require a full sentence utterance rather than a one-word response (*Can you tell me more about that? What else did you learn?*).

Teachers switch to other forms of input as needed. In addition to varying their presentation of content, teachers can offer other options for input, such as visual aids, stories and examples, role playing, and texts at different readability levels, to ease comprehension. Teachers might also provide the same information in both auditory and written form to appeal to both visual and auditory learners. Including peer review sessions in writing classes is another way to provide feedback and input for learners.

Teachers adapt the task to learner proficiency levels. Instructors may change a task to reduce the language load, as appropriate to the learners. Additionally, they may adjust the product of the learning task so that learners are able to demonstrate learning in a variety of ways: projects, group tasks, tests, demonstrations, and so on. Assessments can also be varied to accommodate learners. Tools such as portfolios, rubrics, and oral language reporting provide a picture of an ESP learner's academic growth. However, in all ESP contexts, instructors must be careful to balance task adaptation that allows learners to experience a measure of success with use of authentic tasks that indicate the performance standard that learners will be held to in their future academic, occupational, or professional careers.

Teachers scaffold to provide equitable access to content for all learners. Scaffolding has been defined as the *temporary* structures that teachers use to support learning. Scaffolding supports learners in developing both increased language proficiency and higher-order thinking skills.

Lesson objectives both support and challenge learners when they are scaffolded to increase comprehensibility. Scaffolds come in many different forms and often change as learner proficiency advances. They can be used in tandem to provide higher levels of support. For example, learners who have been paired to read a text together can be given a graphic organizer to help them summarize the main concepts. In general, scaffolds fall into two main categories: material supports and social supports. A sampling of these supports appears in Table 3.3.

Table 3.3 Scaffolding types: Material support and social support

	Scaffolding types
Material support	• Graphic organizers • Diagrams, tables, and charts • Pictures and illustrations • Sentence frames • Advance organizers • Outlines • Structured notes • Two-column charts (e.g., main ideas on left, supporting details on right) • English-to-English dictionaries • Learner dictionaries • Translation dictionaries • Word source software • Alternative and modified texts • Home language texts
Social support	• Small-group learning • Interactively structured conversations • Cooperative learning structures • Group work with designated roles • Pair work • Study groups • Interpreter or cultural informant • Tutoring opportunities • Writing centers • Other campus resources

In addition to these scaffolding types, learning strategies can provide scaffolding for learners who use them to help organize their learning, focus on aspects of language, determine the meaning of unfamiliar words, and memorize. Table 3.4 provides a sampling of such learning strategies.

Table 3.4 Learning strategy scaffolds

	Learning strategies that scaffold learning
Metacognitive and cognitive strategies	• Note taking • Selective listening and reading • Summarizing • Organizational planning • Effective memorization • Prediction • Advance organization • Annotating • Monitoring comprehension
Vocabulary strategies	• Making personal vocabulary logs • Grouping and categorizing words • Visualization • Analysis of word parts • Deducing meaning from context and part of speech • Self-assessment • Substituting a known word for an unknown one • Building word families • Using word lists and glossaries

Principle 5. Monitor and Assess Learner Language Development

Leonida Vizcarra teaches an English for Nursing course in the Philippines. Most of the learners want to practice nursing in the United States. One of her learners does well with her written work, but her spoken language is more limited in both pronunciation and vocabulary. Leonida and the other learners struggle to understand her when she speaks.

Adult English learners advance to differing levels of language proficiency in varied ways depending on their previous language education, culture, and a myriad of other factors. Some learners are comfortable with speaking English even if they can speak only haltingly and ungrammatically. Others wait until they are sure of being understood and certain of their grammatical competence, which usually means they talk very little despite a higher language skill. Constant monitoring and assessment, built into daily instruction, will provide the best evidence for language growth.

PRACTICE 5A Teachers monitor learner errors.

By interacting frequently with learners, instructors can acquire a great deal of information about their progress. This is one main reason that teachers should offer a variety of opportunities for learners to talk with each other and with the teacher in class. Observing learner-learner interactions and participating in learner-teacher ones provides information about individual error patterns as well as global ones that multiple learners are making. Teachers can record their observations in an anecdotal way or using a checklist to determine whether and when to address them and to monitor progress toward the use of correct forms.

Examples of Practice 5a

Teachers take note of errors to provide appropriate feedback to learners. Sometimes learners' errors are simply mistakes caused by lack of attention or lack of competence. Other errors are developmental, indicating that the learner has incomplete learning about the features of English. Some errors involve interference from the first language, such as incorrect word order or cognate words. Instructors should be aware of error causation and provide appropriate remediation and/or feedback. They need not address developmental errors related to language features not yet learned, but they can model correct speech or written text.

Teachers should be aware of and respect learners' preferences for error correction. For example, do they want to be told right after they make the error so they can restate? Or, do they prefer to be told individually and not in front of others in class? In addition, teachers should make careful judgments about when error correction is appropriate in relation to both the immediate learning task and the larger goals of instruction. For example, if learners are engaged in an oral communication task and the error that the instructor observes is not hindering communication, then correction can wait because it would interfere with task completion. Similarly, if the purpose of the task is to simulate the learners' target academic or professional environment, where error correction will not take place, then the teacher should defer correction until a later time so as not to compromise task authenticity.

Teachers reteach when errors indicate that learners misunderstood or learned the material incorrectly. When errors indicate that learners have not grasped a key point or have understood it incompletely, teachers should plan for reteaching and additional practice. This could involve presenting a mini-lesson on the topic for the whole class or working with a small group of learners who need the support.

PRACTICE 5B **Teachers provide ongoing feedback effectively and strategically.**

Effective feedback has defined characteristics. To be constructive, a teacher's oral feedback in response to a learner's error is best modulated in delivery and tone, whether it is presented in class in front of others or one-on-one during an individual conference. Teachers determine feedback on the basis of their observations of learner performance. The feedback can be positive or corrective. It is important that feedback be specific and related to what learners are doing well in addition to what they can improve. Teachers also may need to vary their feedback types depending on the cultural backgrounds of their learners.

Examples of Practice 5b

Teachers use specific feedback. As mentioned in Practice 2b, praise is often global, but criticism is specific. The more specific teachers can be about learners' accomplishments and errors, the better learners can build on their strengths and work to improve. Specific feedback that highlights errors leads to better performance than general feedback. Modeling is one effective way of providing specific feedback. The instructor may provide the model through demonstration, or may show videos or authentic situations. Assignments and presentations can be modeled before they are assigned, and the models used for comparison afterward. Demonstrations are also helpful in showing how to perform at a high level. For projects, rubrics can be effective in identifying the specific characteristics of success, as long as the rating criteria are explained to learners in advance.

In ESP instruction, where the teacher is not familiar with the content of the learners' target academic discipline, professional field, or occupational domain and where learners are carrying out authentic tasks that simulate work in those arenas, feedback from a content specialist can also be extremely valuable. Such feedback can give learners a detailed picture of the ways in which they met the expectations of the target context and the aspects that need further attention.

Teachers give actionable, just-in-time feedback. Learners are more able to use feedback if they receive it while they are actively working on a task, especially when the feedback is encouraging and specific to aspects of the work that they can understand and change. Rather than delaying feedback until the product is finished, teachers can embed feedback checkpoints into assignments, when learners are highly motivated to attend to guidance and to act on the teacher's recommendations.

Teachers align their feedback strategy to learners' proficiency levels and individual preferences. A feedback focus is helpful for both teacher and learner, so some instructors determine the feedback focus in consultation with the learner. Teachers ask adult English learners what goals they are working on and what specifically they would like feedback on. The focus is defined, and a time period is determined for observation (such as for speech in a particular setting) or review (such as for written work). When possible, flipped lessons or classes are beneficial because with this method learners spend more time working with and receiving feedback from the teacher and peers in class. However, the flipped classroom model may be difficult for instructors in EOP contexts to implement, because adults in occupational learning rarely have time for reading or practice outside of class.

Although feedback is an important tool of language teachers and research supports its use, it only makes sense for adults in the form that they like to receive it and can make use of it. This applies to both oral and written feedback. Some learners struggle when responding to large amounts of feedback, especially if they consider the feedback to be negative. However, most learners are open to positive feedback—the type that specifically points out what they are doing correctly and encourages them to continue the beneficial behavior. Separating positive and negative feedback helps ESP learners concentrate more clearly on what is already being done correctly and what can be done better.

Teachers use a feedforward approach. The feedforward approach shifts the focus, so that instead of examining what the learner did well or not well in an already completed task or assignment, instructor and learner look at what can be improved for the future or in the next assignment based on evidence in the current work. It can be used developmentally to incrementally advance the learner's linguistic abilities.

Teachers use a variety of types of oral corrective feedback. Corrective feedback allows learners an opportunity to notice the differences between their language and the language of the teacher. Oral feedback occurring in teacher-learner interactions is generally one of three main types: explicit corrections, recasts, and prompts for self-repair. Research indicates that output-oriented feedback (where the learner produces the correction) is more effective than input-oriented feedback (where the teacher provides the correction). Prompts are especially beneficial in content-based classrooms. They work well when learners receive feedback on grammatical errors that have been taught and are developmentally appropriate. Prompts push learners to self-repair and have been shown to lead to more accurate output (Lyster & Saito, 2010). The three types of oral feedback are illustrated below:

1. ***Explicit corrections*** occur when the teacher indicates to learners that they have made an error and supplies a correction.
    - Learner: *The plane . . . the plane go straight in the air.*
    - Teacher: *Do you mean the plane went up? We say the plane takes off.*
2. ***Recasts*** occur after learners' utterances. The teacher reformulates all or part of the utterance.
    - Learner: *The plane go straight in the air.*
    - Teacher: *The plane takes off.*
3. ***Prompts for self-repair*** signal learners to attempt to repair an utterance on their own. Such prompts can be of many types: repetitions, direct elicitations, clarification requests, metalinguistic clues, open-ended questions, and non-verbal cues.
    - ***Repetition.*** The teacher repeats the learner's utterance, often with exaggeration or inflection to indicate a problem. (Learner: *The plane goes straight in the air.* Teacher: *Straight in the air?*)
    - ***Elicitation.*** The teacher elicits the correct form by asking specific questions, pausing, or asking for a reformulation. (*How do we say that in English? Do you remember the word we used last week to describe that process?*)
    - ***Clarification request.*** The teacher uses a phrase to indicate that the learner's utterance was not understood. (*Excuse me? I don't understand. Can you tell me again?*)
    - ***Metalinguistic clues.*** The teacher asks questions to indicate that the form of the utterance is not correct, e.g., verb form, plurality. (*You need to use the past tense.*)

- *Open-ended questions.* The teacher asks general questions that allow the learner to select the information that he or she will talk about. (*Tell me what you know about . . . ? What did you discover about . . . ? What can you tell me about . . . ?*)
- *Non-verbal cues.* The teacher's quizzical facial expressions and/or gestures may serve as prompts for self-repair. (Lyster & Saito, 2010)

Teachers use written feedback whenever possible. In written feedback, teachers share their insights, opinions, recommendations, and suggestions, with the goal of helping learners improve their English language skills. Written corrective feedback gives learners a lasting record that can help them reflect on their learning more deeply and develop self-regulation processes. In writing classes, ESP teachers can use a collaborative approach to the writing and revision process that mirrors some of the types of writing activities that learners may do in their future academic courses or professional work. Through collaborative revision, teachers can help learners reflect on the strengths and weaknesses of each draft and ask for specific help in making improvements. Peer editing can function in a similar way in all types of ESP settings.

PRACTICE 5C Teachers use effective formative and summative assessment strategies.

Adult learners who want to enter a university or college setting, as well as those who wish to obtain employment in occupational or professional settings, are often faced with the daunting task of passing one or more standardized tests such as the Test of English as a Foreign Language® (TOEFL), the International English Language Testing System™ (IELTS), the College Board® SAT (Scholastic Achievement Test), or the Graduate Record Examinations® (GRE). Many ESP educators feel that these tests do not accurately reveal what adult learners know or are capable of achieving in their chosen fields, nor do they properly prepare learners for EAP, EPP, or EOP instruction. To obtain a more accurate picture of adult English learners' knowledge, abilities, and progress, many instructors prefer to assess them through classroom-based assessment or placement assessment instruments that mirror instruction and are discrete enough to show the progress being made in the ESP classroom.

Examples of Practice 5c

Teachers use classroom-based assessment to inform teaching and improve learning. The purpose of classroom-based assessment is to gather information regarding learning over time. Classroom-based assessment can inform teaching by helping instructors become better acquainted with their learners' growth in specific skill and performance areas. As a result, it can lead to improvement in the learners' learning experiences and language development.

Examples of classroom-based assessments include teacher observations, teacher-developed tests, comprehension checks, and learner tasks or assignments with associated rubrics (such as writing papers or projects, oral presentations or speeches, solving case study problems, and multimedia products), checklists, surveys/questionnaires, and anecdotal records. Classroom-based assessment is integrated into instruction.

Teachers use testing procedures based on principles of assessment. Basic evaluation principles are that assessments should be fair, reliable, and valid.

- *Fairness* requires that all learners have an equal chance to show what they know and can do. Fairness does not require that all learners are treated in the same way. In fact, for adult English learners, it would be unfair to assess them in the same way as native English speakers. That type of assessment often leads to frustration and failure. However, teachers do need to remind learners that they will be assessed in the same way as English speakers once they enter university classes or professional settings. To achieve some degree of fairness in classroom-based testing, teachers provide scaffolds. They may scaffold a writing assessment, for example, by providing models of learner writing. Consider the following questions to determine whether your classroom assessments are fair:

— *Did the learner sufficiently understand the questions asked?*
— *Does my assessment reflect my instructional practices?*
— *Did I provide appropriate scaffolding?*
— *Have I told learners what I am evaluating and modeled a desired product?*
— *Have I clearly specified the criteria on which the evaluation is based?*
— *Am I evaluating the process, the product, or both?*

- ***Reliability*** indicates that the results of an assessment are consistent over a period of time when scored by different raters. Holistic or analytic scoring of writing samples is reliable when raters are trained in the same techniques and achieve similar scores. Oral language scoring can be more reliable when raters use an observational matrix that is specific enough to provide dependable results.
- ***Validity*** is achieved when instruments measure what they are intended to measure. It is difficult to achieve valid results with English learners on standardized tests, particularly those written in English. Testing products may exhibit cultural or experiential bias toward learners with different life experiences. Moreover, the test results are often influenced by the learner's limited academic language knowledge. Because of this, it is good practice for teachers to collect multiple sources of information about a learner.

Teachers rely on a variety of assessment types to determine learner achievement. Although informal assessments can often be fairer and more valid, formal assessments are required by programs, universities, and educational authorities. Instructors therefore need to give their learners opportunities to prepare for formal assessment through practice and strategy development, and if learners are allowed accommodations on the formal test, the teacher needs to use the same accommodations in the classroom.

However, to obtain a full picture of learners' knowledge, skills, and abilities, instructors need to use multiple types of informal assessment that look at learner proficiency levels and progress through differing lenses. The types of assessment that instructors can use include the following:

- ***Formative assessment*** occurs as teachers gather information about learners' progress and performance during the instructional process. Formative assessment is ongoing, occurs during instruction, and guides the teaching process. Much formative assessment is spontaneous (as learners make errors and teachers note them) and occurs during class. Other formative assessments are conducted to evaluate teaching and learning objectives. They may be graded, marked on a checklist, written as anecdotal notes, recorded as oral speech, or collected through short quizzes, essays, and presentations.
- ***Summative assessment***, in contrast to formative assessment, is usually conducted at the end of a long period of learning (a semester or year) and is more formal in tone. It might also occur at the end of a project or on assignments, such research papers or oral presentations. Standardized testing is an example of summative assessment.

- ***Performance-based portfolios*** give teachers access to multiple writing pieces collected over a period of time. A portfolio may contain different genres of writing and reflect editing and rewriting processes. Consequently, a portfolio can provide an excellent picture of the growth of a learner's language development over time.
- ***Criterion-based rubrics*** are useful tools for assessment and learning. They list the specific criteria used to evaluate a performance or a product and then indicate performance levels on a scoring scale that uses numbers, letters, or other descriptive labels. Rubrics are presented by the teacher prior to the learning experience and provide the learner with clear explanations and examples so that all learners will understand the criteria. Rubrics include models work for grading criteria included on the rubric.

Principle 6. Engage and Collaborate Within a Community of Practice

June Arlena teaches a multi-skills EAP class in Vancouver. To help learners apply the skills taught in the class, June works with a former college classmate, Tomoko Kawasaki, who now teaches English in Japan. June and Tomoko have decided to engage their learners in project-based learning, in which learners will study an aspect of global citizenship in the other country, such as solutions to pollution or the global refugee crisis. June and Tomoko work together to pair learners to meet via Skype and share their acquired knowledge and see what someone living in the other country believes about the topic.

A community of practice, briefly introduced in Chapter 1, consists of people who share a profession and engage with one another in collective learning about that profession to help each other grow professionally. No one can know all there is to know about educating diverse learners, and collectively all together are smarter than one alone (Lave & Wenger, 1991). English language teaching professionals often begin the journey to professionalism by looking outside of their own skill sets and exploring the knowledge base of other teachers in their programs. In this way, they can add to their repertoire of teaching techniques. For example, more experienced ESP teachers can inform newer ones who are moving into EAP, EPP, or EOP teaching about the learners, the goals, and the teaching context. For EAP teachers, the community of practice can also include instructors in other university departments who can provide information on the vocabulary and content that adult learners will face when they enter university classes. In EOP settings, in addition to other EOP teachers the community of practice can include human resources professionals, managers, and others concerned with the outcomes of EOP instruction, and in EPP contexts it can include native-English-speaking and nonnative-English-speaking professionals who can advise on the expectations and requirements of the field.

PRACTICE 6A Teachers are fully engaged in their profession.

Although all teachers would like to believe that they are fully prepared for the challenges of the profession on the first day of their teaching careers, few really are. The more time that teachers spend engaging with the act of teaching, the more they feel the need to develop and grow to provide the best instruction for their learners. For educators teaching in ESP settings, being fully engaged means both identifying ways to grow as a language teaching professional and finding ways to connect effectively with members of the occupational, professional, and academic fields that their learners hope to enter.

Examples of Practice 6a

Teachers engage in reflective practice to grow professionally. Dewey (1933) discussed reflective practice in his exploration of experience, interaction, and reflection; and later Schon (1990) enlarged on the notion by defining reflective practice as the process through which professionals learn from their experiences and gain insights into themselves and their practice. Schon differentiated between reflection *in* action and reflection *on* action. Reflection in action occurs when teachers reflect on a teaching or learning behavior as it occurs. Reflection on action involves reflecting after the event: reviewing, analyzing, and evaluating the situation.

Reflection in action calls for an instructor to do self-observation while teaching, monitoring the choices made and then recording notes on completion of the lesson. This is the skill of critical inquiry. Some teachers use a journal for daily reflections. Others write anecdotally with the idea of sharing the experience with a peer.

Reflection on action requires that teachers have solitary time to think about the lesson and to reflect on what occurred, why it happened, how the teaching behavior related to theory or background knowledge, and what ideas it might suggest for future teaching situations. This is the skill of self-reflection. During this time, teachers examine their assumptions of everyday practice and evaluate them. The process can be distilled into three essential questions:

- *What did I do?*
- *How did it go?*
- *What did I learn?*

Reflective practice, called critical reflection, can lead to positive professional growth: "Unless teachers develop the practice of critical reflection, they stay trapped in unexamined judgments, interpretations, assumptions, and expectations. Approaching teaching as a reflective practitioner involves fusing personal beliefs and values into a professional identity" (Larrivee, 2000, p. 293). Teachers who engage in cyclical critical reflection become teachers who constantly test hypotheses about teaching and learning and experiment with these hypotheses in light of the context of the learning and the learners who are affected. In this way, these teachers are constantly renewed and steadily increase their professional competence.

Teachers participate in continuous learning and ongoing professional development. The challenges of teaching and the diversity of ESP learners increase every day. The effective teacher's response to these challenges is to be continually working toward professional involvement and lifelong learning. Initially, individual interest will guide engagement in learning—a love of music, a connection with a profession through family or friends, an interest in other cultural groups, or a critical shortage of behavior management techniques.

Through personal learning networks, instructors can question, share experiences, design workshops, develop study groups, pursue online training, write curricula, and talk about classroom experiences: What I did today, and what I learned as a result. These conversations are rare due to time constraints and work necessary outside the classroom. But when they do happen, they lead to the reflection and development that are so necessary to becoming a better teacher.

Through participation in professional development associations and opportunities, such as reading educational blogs, watching webinars, or perusing websites, instructors can stay abreast of best practices. Attending conferences at local, regional, national, and international levels and participating in organization listservs can provide a wealth of teaching resources and ideas. Teachers can consider joining a number of professional organizations, such as TESOL International Association and its affiliates around the world, Asia TEFL (Asia Teaching English as a Foreign Language), IATEFL (International Association of Teachers of English as a Foreign Language), CCCC (Conference on College Composition and Communication), AAAL (American Association for Applied Linguistics), ACTFL (American Council on the Teaching of Foreign Languages), and IAWE (International Association of World Englishes). As a member, an instructor can become involved with one of the organization's committees and can present at local, state, or national conferences or sponsored academies and symposia. Teachers can also read and write for the publications of these organizations to get new insights and exchange ideas.

In addition, teachers can pursue learning options in specific skill areas related to teaching—technology, curriculum development, or assessment, for example. They can take online courses and webinars, or apply for a grant, fellowship, or award to do language research or pursue a graduate degree. The list is long, but lifelong learning takes time. Instructors need to invest their own time, and often their own money, to become dynamic and effective teachers of adult English language learners.

PRACTICE 6B **Teachers collaborate with one another to co-plan and co-teach.**

Many programs have a curriculum teachers need to follow and sometimes a textbook may be shared by all the teachers teaching the same course. As a result, collaboration can benefit teachers who teach the same course. They can share ideas, lessons, and methods. June and Tomoko illustrate this practice in the earlier vignette.

Examples of Practice 6b

Teachers meet with colleagues regularly. Time is the most valuable commodity for teachers. Teachers' schedules rarely permit them to have lengthy meetings with department colleagues, or to find opportunities for mutual planning on a course or within a program. In spite of this challenge, instructors who can make the time to meet with other teachers can better ensure their learners' success in developing the language and skills they will need to be successful in their chosen academic or professional paths. These planning opportunities permit teachers to become aware of the what their colleagues do in their classrooms and share ideas about managing the challenges they face. They also allow teachers to share information about learners they share or have had in other classes previously. Some programs are able to schedule shared planning time for teachers.

Teachers develop and strengthen relationships with program colleagues who can serve as mentors. When teaching in a new setting or teaching a course for the first time, if possible an instructor should schedule time to meet with a colleague who has taught the class before. Such meetings can provide insight to the course objectives and the types of learners likely to be in the class, and can offer ideas for lesson plans.

Teachers meet with industry and subject matter experts in the professional and occupational fields that their learners wish to pursue. Finding time to meet with professionals in subject-matter fields can be even more challenging than finding time for teacher-teacher interactions. However, such meetings are essential for teachers in all types of instruction, because they provide the input that teachers must have if they are to design courses and instructional activities that meet the needs and goals of their learners. Since instructors are not themselves experts in the professional or occupational fields that their adult learners hope to enter, they need guidance from subject matter experts who can describe the modes and levels of language use that are typical of their fields, as well as the types of oral and written tasks and texts that characterize it. This input enables instructors to create authentic learning materials and activities for their learners.

Teachers confer with professors or teachers whose courses EAP learners will enter after leaving the second language classroom. Instructors should consider sitting in on classes or asking professors about their classes to guide lesson planning and ensure that the class teaches skills that will help adult learners prepare for what they will encounter. If meetings are not possible, instructors can request syllabuses or find samples online. Such information can help inform course objectives and determine what authentic material might be helpful to include in lessons.

A Look Back and a Look Ahead

The 6 Principles that Chapter 3 has described are the basic tenets that guide the English for specific purposes profession. Some of these principles may overlap with the guidelines for TESOL professionals in other settings; others may overlap with how professionals teach native speakers.

Taken as a whole, however, they outline the distinctive responsibilities and skills of all professionals who teach adult learners in EOP, EPP, and EAP courses and programs. They concisely state what exemplary teaching of learners in these contexts requires teachers to do.

Principle 1. *Know Your Learners.* Teachers gather information about each learner's background, particularly those aspects that are consequential for their language development. These aspects include learners' native languages and cultures, their levels of English language development, and all the factors that can support or hinder their second language development. Teachers also identify each learner's English language learning objectives and career, professional, or academic goals, and develop an understanding of the language and related skills that the learner will need in order to achieve those larger goals.

Principle 2. *Create Conditions for Language Learning.* Teachers make the teaching setting a place where learners are motivated to learn, practice, and take risks with language. Teachers work to secure all the essential conditions of second language acquisition, draw on beneficial conditions, and set high expectations for their learners.

Principle 3. *Design High Quality Lessons for Language Development.* Teachers know what learners can do with the current learning objectives and what they need to learn next. Then teachers determine course objectives, plan how they will convey information, promote rich course conversations, decide on tasks that are meaningful and encourage authentic language practice, and explicitly teach learning strategies and critical thinking skills.

Principle 4. *Adapt Lesson Delivery as Needed.* Teachers monitor their learners' comprehension, adjusting lectures or materials, differentiating instruction, and scaffolding tasks according to learners' English language proficiency levels. They make decisions about adjustments during lesson delivery on the basis of learner responses and actions and a solid understanding of the second language development process.

Principle 5. *Monitor and Assess Learner Language Development.* Teachers gauge how well learners are progressing in English, note and evaluate the types of errors that learners make, offer strategic feedback, and use a variety of assessment types to measure learner outcomes.

Principle 6. *Engage and Collaborate Within a Community of Practice.* Teachers understand that they can serve learners better when they work together. Teaching learners requires that teachers be part of a community of practice within their school and the broader education community that affords them access to ongoing professional development. Teachers should collaborate with colleagues so they understand the language and demands of the setting in which they teach, and with subject matter experts in the fields that their learners hope to enter so they can create authentic materials and tasks that will support learners in achieving their goals.

Each of The 6 Principles challenges teachers of adult English learners to develop professionally. The Appendix provides a self-assessment checklist for teachers to use to evaluate their own implementation of The 6 Principles and supporting practices. Programs are changing rapidly, learners are increasingly diverse, and, as professionals, teachers must also change and grow while holding fast to those principles that they know will lead to excellence and achievement for the learners.

Chapter 4 builds on the practices described in Principle 6 and highlights the ways in which teachers of adult English learners can be resources for other educators. The chapter moves beyond this particular function to explain how teachers can be agents of change and advocates for their learners.

Additional resources for this book are available at www.the6principles.org/eap-esp.

4 ESTABLISHING A CULTURE OF SHARED RESPONSIBILITY

Adult English learners benefit from being surrounded by a supportive community that takes responsibility for fostering their success. Such a community includes a wide base of professionals who have differing roles in helping the adult learners achieve their goals in academic, professional and occupational contexts. These professionals may form a community of practice that functions as a support system for these adult learners.

The phrase "community of practice" describes a group of individuals who engage in a process of collective learning as they practice their profession. These practitioners, each with their own skill sets, actively share knowledge, resources, experiences, and orientations to their work. They also build relationships that enhance their collaborative efforts. As a community of practice, practitioners in an educational institution can collectively move their programs forward to ensure an equitable, high-quality education for all learners (Theoharis & O'Toole, 2011). Each professional can advance his or her own knowledge and skills in the collaborative process of supporting the learners. This in turn furthers the mission of the institution.

For adult learners who are seeking to strengthen their English language skills in order to pursue higher education or enter a professional or occupational field, having a community of practice that shares responsibility for their progress can be critical. In occupational settings, this may mean a willingness on the part of management to budget for customized English for occupational purposes (EOP) training, as well as flex-time for employees who need to attend that training or opportunities for potential employees to participate in it. It may also entail establishment of an in-house mentoring system in which supervisors or peers with stronger English language skills provide one-on-one support for those working to develop their English. Similarly, in professional context (English for professional purposes, or EPP), support may take the form of customized training in key skills such as writing summary reports and making formal presentations. In international work it may also include a strengths-based approach to team building, in which English learners are valued as team members because of their familiarity with another language and culture, sharing that expertise and receiving input that helps them develop their English language skills as team members work together on projects.

In academic contexts, the situation is quite different, because many institutions in non-English-speaking countries are delivering entire college and university training programs using English as the medium of instruction (EMI) and because the number of international students enrolled in higher education degree programs in English-speaking countries, and thus needing English for academic purposes (EAP), has increased dramatically. It takes the whole university community to support the academic development of these learners.

This chapter focuses primarily on academic contexts, including university EAP programs, intensive English programs (IEPs), and private language institutes (PLIs), and addresses those in key roles: institutional leaders, program administrators, academic faculty, and guidance and academic counselors—all of whom contribute directly to the overall success of programs and services designed for adult English learners.[1] Other personnel, such as recruiters, international student officers, service staff, admissions counselors and curriculum developers, also contribute to the success of adult English learners at one or more points in their educational trajectory. Because key professionals closely support the type of exemplary teaching that this book describes, this chapter extends the discussion of The 6 Principles to outline how those beyond the English language classroom can support in meaningful ways. Not every principle is relevant for every group, so this chapter examines only those that apply most directly to each one.

Chapter 4 provides recommendations for the following groups:

- Institutional leaders in academic programs and PLIs
- English for Specific Purposes program administrators, including those in IEPs and PLIs
- Academic faculty in all content areas
- Academic and guidance counselors

This chapter explores the roles played by members of these groups which, taken together, provide a full picture of a culture of shared responsibility for adult English learners. Those who are members of one or more of these groups can focus on the relevant parts and examine the recommendations for their role(s). Those who find that they lack information or skills pertaining to any of the points presented can work to build those competencies and strengthen their practice so that they can contribute fully to promoting the success of adults in EAP, EPP, and EOP programs. They can make learning about adult English learners a professional goal that they pursue in one or more of these ways:

- Reaching out to local colleges and universities
- Attending TESOL International or TESOL International affiliate conferences
- Joining the Higher Education, English for Specific Purposes, and/or Program Administrators interest sections and/or the Intensive English Program professional learning network of TESOL
- Joining online communities focused on English learner education
- Participating in online courses
- Exploring websites designed for teachers of adult English learners

They can also organize committees and study groups to foster the growth and development of all the professionals who make up their communities of practice. Teachers and program directors might also move their institutions or programs forward by sharing the appropriate sections of this chapter with colleagues. They can also offer to participate in regional committees to improve programs and services.

Institutional Leaders

Dr. Alan Rodriguez is the president of a university set in a small city in central Canada. The university has invested greatly in the recruitment of international students from south and central Asia and has seen the number of enrollments grow from 100 international students to 3,000 over the past five years. Dr. Rodriguez knows first-hand that the success of these students hinges on having sufficient proficiency in English to integrate into the local and academic community. Coming from Colombia, he is particularly sensitive to the challenges they face. He recalls feeling great culture shock in his first days as a student in Canada with limited ability to express himself in English,

---

[1] The content in this chapter may also apply to the language training departments in large multinational corporations. Such companies may have language departments with a cadre of in-house English trainers, both part-time and full-time, a materials development department, and a full time teacher trainer who observes classes, runs workshops, and so on. The department functions as an in-house language school, but limited to in-house clients.

resulting in communication difficulties with classmates and professors. Under his leadership, he has spearheaded a university English learner committee comprised of members from the international student recruitment office, the international students office, the student-learning centre, the ESL pathway program, curriculum designers, and academic faculty to discuss ways to better integrate these students on campus. One of the emerging concerns shared by all is that English learners do not fully participate in class. Professors hold the same expectations for English language learners as native speakers regarding the level and frequency of participation in class. Drawing from the rich experience and expertise within the group, the English learner committee has made recommendations, and now professors incorporate small break-out discussion groups in class, hold more online discussion forums, and use clickers to identify student results instantly to check comprehension in larger lecture halls. These changes have increased successful participation by both international and domestic students.

Institutional leaders in academic and private school settings often serve adult English learners who come from a variety of linguistic and cultural backgrounds. They are learning and using English for academic purposes or for professional/occupational purposes in either the public or private sector.

These programs serve the needs of the learners to perform certain tasks in English. For example, consider a high school graduate from the Middle East who is learning EAP in an IEP for one year. His goal is to enroll in an engineering degree program at an English-medium university in his country. Other examples include a marketing specialist, with five years of work experience, who is polishing her English speaking skills at a PLI to advance her career path; a graduate student from China who is taking an EAP for business graduate course prior to studying international business at a university in Australia; and an airline pilot in Germany who is learning English to communicate more proficiently with air traffic controllers through a company-based EOP program.

Regardless of the context, the pedagogy in The 6 Principles is applicable to all programs. Institutional leaders will need to develop substantial knowledge about adult English learners in order to offer the best instructional programs and empirically based practices to serve them. This section suggests actions that these leaders can take to support those who implement The 6 Principles within these varied contexts.

Institutional Leaders in Academic Programs

Institutional leaders supervising EAP programs likely have many learners who are either international students in an ESL context or studying in English-medium schools in an EFL context. Given the complexity of both of these settings, adult English learners face immense challenges in terms of linguistic knowledge and cultural adaptations. Acquiring proficiency in English is the first step for them, as English is the gateway to academic and career development. Therefore it is the leader's responsibility to ensure that the appropriate systems and resources are in place to support these learners in developing their proficiency in English and to smooth their transition into their academic and professional/occupational programs (DePetro Orlando, 2016). Whether students are learning English in a pre-professional or a professional program, the strategic directions that institutional leaders take will inform policies and procedures to fully support their integration and maximize their contributions to a community of knowledge. Some of the following suggestions extend beyond language teaching but are crucial in supporting learners in achieving their goals.

Principle 1. *Know Your Learners*
- View adult English learners not from a deficit perspective, but as a serviceable group of learners with skills and knowledge who are responsibly factored into strategic planning decisions at the school, from ethical recruitment to student support, rights, responsibilities, and policies.

- Ensure that the institutional mission statement promotes values of global citizenship and inclusivity, drawing on the diversity of a multicultural student population that enriches the teaching and learning experience for all faculty and students.
- Take responsible action by consulting with those who work closely with adult English learners in order to take informed decisions on how the school can intervene to provide the best overall experience for them.
- Include academic program administrators, instructors, and support staff in high-level conversations regarding decisions related to adult English learners.
- Include pre-academic entry English language program administrators, instructors, and students in the wider activities and organizations at the school.
- Leverage the rich cultural and linguistic diversity of the student body to promote the development of global competencies to give all students the tools they will need to live and work in a globalized world.
- Provide space to adult English learners to act as cultural ambassadors, sharing their diverse perspectives and experiences with faculty, students, and staff.
- Create opportunities for adult English learners to be active community members who contribute to the intellectual and cultural growth of the campus.
- Avoid marginalizing adult English learners and viewing lack of proficiency in English as a learning deficit. Avoid deficit terminology and labelling within registrar systems.
- Put systems in place to educate faculty and staff on language proficiency development.

Principle 2. *Create Conditions for Language Learning*

- Provide support and freedom for faculty to make their courses more accessible to their adult English learners, such as by working with an ESL or EFL expert on campus, internationalizing course content to draw in more participation from English learners, or seeking training in more inclusive teaching pedagogies.
- Support the integration of adult English learners on campus, and demonstrate an openness to their cultural backgrounds by providing opportunities for them to establish culturally representative student groups.
- Provide multilingual student services on campus, hiring bi/multilingual healthcare professionals, academic advisors, admission counselors, student mentors, and others.
- Hire bilingual, multilingual, and minority staff to work across all levels in the institution.

Principle 3. *Design High-Quality Lessons for Language Development*

- Ensure that support departments on campus provide continual learning support to adult English learners throughout their language training and academic studies.
- Employ the expertise of an ESL or EFL specialist in the campus teaching and learning department to provide faculty support.
- Encourage collaborations between English teaching and content-area teaching faculty to design course content adaptable for adult English learners.

Principle 5. *Monitor and Assess Learner Language Development*

- Establish realistic language proficiency cut scores on standardized tests for admission to the school to ensure that learners' English language skills are at the level necessary to successfully perform in their academic studies.

- Ensure that the pre-university pathway program curriculum appropriately assesses academic and language skill development to help learners transition into their academic studies.
- Track academic achievement with language program scores to ensure that learners have enough time to properly obtain a level of language proficiency in which they can successfully cope with the rigor of academic studies.

Principle 6. *Engage and Collaborate Within a Community of Practice*

This is the way we do things around here.

The vignette earlier in this chapter highlighted a common observation from faculty that adult English learners do not fully participate in class. Dr. Rodriguez's initiative to establish a university committee that draws stakeholders from all areas on campus that touch upon the academic and social integration of adult English learners is a prime example of a solution-oriented community of practice. Every institutional leader can consider forming a committee for a similar or other relevant purpose to encourage more collaboration. Table 4.1 highlights the contribution of each member on the university committee and the takeaways which will in turn help them do their jobs better and assist in meeting the objectives of The 6 Principles.

Table 4.1   Community of Practice

Member	Contribution to the group	Takeaway from the experience
EAP Coordinator	Chantal is the EAP coordinator of the English pathway program. She has been mandated to strike this committee to improve the student experience of English language learners at her university.	As the point person on campus, she has a better understanding of the student experience and can provide reports to her manager, who reports to the Dean of Students.
International recruiter	Roger travels extensively in the learners' home countries and is able to provide perspective and context on learners' expected and perceived behaviors.	During his recruitment trips, he can better communicate expectations learners and their teachers and advisors. In turn, learners will be better prepared if they are coached on expectations.
International student officer	Antoine organizes support groups on campus for international students. Learners often mention they feel inadequately prepared to participate in class, so become discouraged and frustrated.	He can address cultural issues related to participation and direct learners to support services on campus that can assist them in developing these skills.
Student learning specialist	Jen provides strategies to faculty to foster student participation. She suggests the use of online forums because they give learners more time to formulate questions and answers. She also finds forums effective in making learners feel more connected to each other, which will eventually help them participate in class.	She is working with Antoine to develop a PDF study guide for students entitled "Professor Expectations—Speak Up!"

(continued)

Table 4.1	Community of Practice *(continued)*	
Member	Contribution to the group	Takeaway from the experience
ESL pathway program instructor	Derek explains that adult English learners may feel intimidated volunteering an answer or asking questions in a big lecture setting, and suggests using instructional strategies common in EAP classes, such as breakout discussion groups of 2–3 learners.	He develops activities for learners to strengthen critical thinking and questioning skills based on Bloom's taxonomy.
Curriculum developer	Frank is the go-to person on campus for curricular design and pedagogy, and he suggests using resources on campus to facilitate student participation, such as online forums through the learning management system and clickers recently purchased for faculty use.	He develops a short video tutorial for faculty with strategies to increase learner participation. The video is archived on the university website for future reference.

Institutional Leaders in Private Language Institutes

Aguascalientes in north central Mexico is the largest growing car industry in the country. The automotive industry has brought economic development and employment to the area, and an essential need for workers to learn English to communicate with the auto companies' plant managers from Korea and Japan. The companies provide English language training to Spanish-speaking workers who require English in their work environment. At one company, a PLI provides training in the four skills—reading, writing, listening, and speaking—and on career-specific vocabulary (car parts, safety features, manufacturing, and so on). The administration respects the workers' work-life balance. Workers are paid to attend class during regular work hours to encourage participation and achievement. The workers are motivated to learn and appreciate the company's investment in their professional development. "I'm lucky to have a good job and opportunities to grow in my workplace. I like to communicate with my manager Yoon and talk about soccer."

—Juan Ramirez, process technician

The leader of a PLI that teaches EAP in pre-university or college programs, or English to professionals who need the language for their careers, needs an understanding of second language acquisition and of the different contexts in which people need to learn English for their studies or professions. English for specific purposes, whether for academic, professional, or occupational settings, may include some general English language training but differs from general English in that it has a specialized focus on vocabulary and tasks specific to the context. The range of learner needs and goals will differ from one context to another and may require tailor-made language courses. It is therefore important to hire ESP teachers who can understand the learning context and provide targeted instruction.

Principle 1. *Know Your Learners*

- Determine learners' goals and expectations. Employ a needs assessment tool to ensure that the program is suited for their language needs and level.
- Meet with industry groups to elicit language needs (and possibly cross-cultural training) for their companies.

Principle 2. *Create Conditions for Language Learning*

- Determine the proficiency level of the learners to ensure that each one can meet the learning objectives.
- Group learners with others at the same level of proficiency to encourage progression and participation.
- Select contextually relevant and appropriate materials for the learners to use in achieving their linguistic goals.
- Provide support to instructors who wish to design tailored courses to meet the needs of the learners and the industry.
- Provide or encourage staff to seek training on current teaching pedagogies.
- Hire qualified teachers and bilingual or multilingual staff.

ESP Program Administrators

In our EAP program, our administration places great value on excellence in teaching and student-centered learning. As part of the job interview process, we ask teaching candidates to prepare and deliver a 20-minute mini-lesson on a teaching concept from the course syllabus. The interview begins with basic questions and is followed by the candidate simulating a class to the hiring panel, which consists of a program administrator and two senior EAP instructors. Doing this gives us a clear indication of the teacher's level of professionalism, preparation, and performance. It also provides an opportunity to ask questions and provide feedback to the instructor. The mini-lesson helps us determine which candidates are not a good fit for our program and suggests areas for them to improve their pedagogy.

The role of an ESP program administrator is to support adult English learners and their teachers so that the learners can acquire the proficiency level needed to achieve their academic or professional goals. This role covers a wide range of areas that directly influence the success of programs and courses. Pedagogical decisions, materials, curricula, hiring, teacher professional development, learner support, campus integration, and advocacy for learners are only some of the responsibilities that program administrators deal with on a daily basis. Intentional planning and leadership will help a program realize The 6 Principles and will pave the way for successful integration of learners into their academic, professional, and occupational lives.

Principle 1: *Know Your Learners*

Samara is the English language coordinator at a language school in Beirut. Many of the students in her school are Syrian refugees, living in Lebanon and studying English to pursue undergraduate degree programs at American satellite universities in the Middle East. The school is a welcoming environment for students—each morning in the "student hub" hot tea and fresh fruit are served while students connect to wi-fi, charge their phones, and use the computer terminals and printers. In collaboration with some of the target universities, Samara has developed an ambassador program for the students. Each student pairs up with a university student in the American system and they connect through videoconferencing, using WhatsApp, Skype, or FaceTime once a week. These meetings provide authentic language practice outside of the classroom and an opportunity for students to share their experiences, ask questions about plans, and develop friendships. Adi, a student from Damascus, said, "I look forward to coming to school each day. I depend on the comfort of the school, the friendly faces, and the community feeling to lift my spirit. I left behind my country, friends, and family. Now I have a new friend, Justin in America, who is teaching me about what to expect in my mechanical engineering degree program."

- Learn about the backgrounds of the learners in the program. Are they IEP, immigrants, or refugee students? Have they lived and studied in this country and are now learning English for a particular job? Understanding where they come from and where they want to go will clarify the most effective ways to support them in their daily learning paths.
- Identify the learners' academic, cultural, and social strengths.
- For academic settings, find out what potential challenges the learners will face in integrating into a new culture. If they are international students, how are their educational systems different from those of the host country? Asking these questions will help to ensure that the program and student services are responsive to the learners.
- Stay connected to the learners on a day-to-day basis to monitor how things are going with them. Meet them at orientation for a first touch point and follow up during breaks or lunch for informal chit-chat.

Principle 2: *Create Conditions for Language Learning*

- Adopt an appropriate, valid, and reliable multi-pronged approach to language placement test procedures for the language program. Placement tests evaluate the learner's performance in reading, writing, speaking, and listening skills, vocabulary, grammar, and/or other areas (see Table 4.2 for commercial placement tests). Placing learners into the appropriate levels creates a positive condition for language learning that leads to greater learner satisfaction and success in meeting learning goals.

Table 4.2 Common Language Placement Tests

Test	Measures	Links	Context
iBT TOEFL	R/W/S/L	www.ets.org/toefl	EOP/EPP/EAP
IELTS	R/W/S/L	www.ielts.org	EOP/EPP/EAP
COMPASS	R/W	www.compassprep.com	EAP
ACCUPLACER	R/W	www.accuplacer.collegeboard.org	EAP
Duolingo	R/W/S/L	www.englishtest.duolingo.com	EOP/EPP/EAP

- Support teachers in conducting diagnostic tests to validate placement and to discover the strengths and weaknesses of the learners so they can design effective instruction. Diagnostic tests should consist of some productive language activities, such a group discussion to assess speaking or a short writing passage. Not all learners are great test-takers, so the diagnostics conducted on the first day of the course may also result in moving some learners to a higher or lower level. Scheduling in some diagnostic testing in the first days of class is an effective way to make sure that learners are in the right place to learn. Table 4.3 offers guidance for placement.

Table 4.3   Three Steps to Effective Language Placement

Steps	Step 1	Step 2	Step 3
	Placement Test (in-house, online, standardized test score)	In-class diagnostics and teacher observations	Teacher validation and level confirmation
Notes	As a preliminary measure, adopt a placement test to do a first placement of the student. Ensure alignment between test performance indicators and the levels in the program. Ensure that the test is valid and aligns with program and level outcomes.	On the first day of class, have teachers do a variety of assessment tasks within classroom activities to test the performance of the learners. Use of an authentic setting may influence learner performance.	With the data collected from the in-class diagnostics, the teacher can then more precisely confirm whether the learner has been placed in the appropriate group.

- Develop the program based on the standards for language teaching specific to your context, such as the Common European Framework Reference for Languages, or the Canadian Language Benchmarks (see Table 2.1 for references).
- Hire highly qualified ESL or EFL instructors, bilingual educators, and language teaching specialists with an educational background and work experience in Teaching English as a Second/Foreign Language who possess the personal and professional qualities needed to teach learners effectively. Provide new hires with training in the program's curriculum, methodology, and materials through mentoring by seasoned teachers.
- Hire culturally sensitive office staff with experience in working with a diverse population. Seek candidates who demonstrate key characteristics, such as good listening skills, friendliness, patience, kindness, and generosity. An important characteristic is empathy. Candidates who have learned a second language themselves will be able to relate to the learners' experiences.
- Set standards and performance criteria for instructors to ensure coherence in teaching across the department or program. See Table 4.4 as an example.
- Use standards to evaluate the effectiveness of instructors' teaching. Provide feedback and performance reviews.
- Plan professional development activities for instructors to transform their weaknesses into strengths and to keep up with emerging technologies, pedagogies, and other activities related to building success with learners.

Table 4.4 Standards for ESL/EFL Teachers of Adults

Standard	Description
Planning	Teachers plan instruction to promote learning and meet learner goals, and modify plans to assure learner engagement and achievement.
Instructing	Teachers create supportive environments that engage all learners in purposeful learning and promote respectful classroom interactions.
Assessing	Teachers recognize the importance of and are able to gather and interpret information about learning and performance to promote the continuous intellectual and linguistic development of each learner. Teachers use knowledge of student performance to make decisions about planning and instruction "on the spot" and for the future. Teachers involve learners in determining what will be assessed and provide constructive feedback to learners, based on assessments of their learning.
Identity and Context	Teachers understand the importance of who learners are and how their communities, backgrounds, and goals shape learning and expectations of learning. Teachers recognize how context contributes to identity formation and therefore influences learning. Teachers use this knowledge of identity and settings in planning, instructing, and assessing.
Language Proficiency	Teachers demonstrate that they possess sufficient proficiency in the language of instruction given the level of their students.
Content	Teachers understand that language learning is most likely to occur when learners are trying to use the language for genuine communicative purposes. Teachers understand that the content of the language course is the language that learners need in order to discuss, listen to, read, and write about a subject or content area. Teachers design their lessons to help learners acquire the language they need to successfully communicate in the subject or content areas.
Commitment and Professionalism	Teachers continue to develop their understanding of the relationship between second language teaching and learning through the community of English language teaching professionals, the broader teaching community, and the community at large. This knowledge, in turn, informs and changes both the teachers and the communities.

Adapted from *Standards for ESL and EFL Teachers of Adults* (TESOL, 2008).

Like The 6 Principles, the *Standards for ESL/EFL Teachers of Adults* (TESOL, 2008) can benefit program administrators as well as their EAP, EPP, and EOP educators and teacher trainers, because each standard is presented with a synopsis of empirical research, performance indicators, and real-life vignettes. Each component helps guide instructors to identify effective instruction and practices to improve performance.

Principle 5: *Monitor and Assess Learner Language Development*

- Adopt a three-fold holistic definition of learner success that goes beyond academic achievement to include interpersonal relationships and cultural integration for learners. Create conditions within the program through extracurricular activities, mentoring activities, and campus community activities for learners to develop relationships with one another and with other students on campus to help them feel more at ease.
- Know the curriculum. Being well versed and knowledgeable in the program curriculum will help an administrator make informed decisions and create more collaborative work

relationships with instructors (eliminating us vs. them). By having a deep familiarity with the curriculum, an administrator can support teachers and staff who work with learners.
- Collect performance data from instructors on their learners and make adjustments to program curriculum if required.
- Adopt an annual review of program outcomes and make revisions based on learner needs, assessment data, program evaluation, and teacher feedback. Integrate revisions into target teacher professional development activities; self-assess and revise initial instructional goals with a focus on improving outcomes for the learners (Cooper, 2017).

Principle 6: *Engage and Collaborate Within a Community of Practice*

"This past summer, as a way of engaging in a culture of shared responsibility for refreshing our evidence-based practices, a few of my colleagues and I formed a book club. Rather than reading a bunch of primary sources, we instead chose to use The 6 Principles for Exemplary Teaching of English Learners by TESOL as a framework for our discussions. Although the authors wrote the book for a K–12 audience, we found the general concepts applicable to our university-based Intensive English Program." (Lacroix, 2018)

- Plan professional development activities in collaboration with instructors. Determine the areas of growth and development together to ensure buy-in and collaboration.
- Keep instructors up to date with the field by sharing and discussing research and informing them of professional development activities on campus or in the community.
- Encourage teachers to belong to professional development organizations such as TESOL International and TESOL affiliates.
- Provide funding opportunities for teachers to attend professional development events.
- Invite teachers to present on projects and activities they are piloting in class.
- Invite members of the school community to discuss services available to English learners.
- Open the program to graduate students who wish to conduct research with adult English learners.

Beantown Language School is a small private language school outside of London, England. A few years ago, they spearheaded a program to support one instructor per year to attend the annual TESOL Convention and Expo. Each year, the school provides a travel grant of $3,000 USD to an instructor who demonstrates leadership, creativity, innovation, and dedication. The condition for the grant is for the instructor to offer professional development through turn-key training to her/his colleagues in multiple sessions called, "What's New at TESOL." In these sessions, the awardee provides handouts from sessions, activities, and information from teaching grammar to technology. These activities have refueled the program with innovation, best practices, and new community connections. In reflecting on his experience, Raj, the awardee from a prior year stated, "I am fortunate to work at a school that values and encourages the development of their teachers."

Academic Faculty

"I hope that they can tell us, whether or not your language is good will not affect your grades. It is whether or not you're serious in learning, your thoughts are clear, if they said this, I'll feel much better. . . . I keep worrying that my language is not good enough and they'd deduct marks (Dan)." (Excerpt from Heng, 2017, p. 839)

Dan has completed his pre-university English language training program and has begun his academic program at a North American university, but his language is still in development. Dan may still make errors with word forms and complex grammatical structures. How much should these errors affect the grading, for example, of a lab report?

Learners like Dan have probably spent the last 6–12 months studying in a pre-university language program and have received instruction in language and academic skills. Up to now, most of the feedback and evaluation has been on language accuracy. In transitioning to an undergraduate program, learners wonder how much professors consider language proficiency in assessment. This may be challenging for adult English learners because evaluation standards often differ from one professor to the next. Some faculty may weigh more of the grading on how well learners communicate their ideas, despite language-related errors, while others may be distracted by non-English-like structures and phrases and downgrade the product.

The professional context is complex for academic faculty today. As competition for top faculty increases, they are being recruited from across the globe to teach in English-speaking countries and in EMI contexts, although they themselves may not hold high levels of English proficiency. In these mixed international settings, adult English learners are likely to struggle to adapt to classroom practices and may not understand the references that faculty make in relation to the content they teach. Some of the content they deliver in their courses can get lost in translation, if it is not tailored to the audience. Furthermore, other academic concerns such as the variety of interpretations of academic integrity and evolving technologies such as machine translations are developing new literacies related to conducting academic work. Faculty members are required to teach diverse learner populations that include adult English learners and to develop inclusive practices within their teaching approaches.

This section can guide academic faculty in their roles as instructors of adult English learners in academic, professional, and occupational programs. Since their area of specialization is not English language teaching for nonnative speakers, this section seeks to support them in helping adult English learners succeed in their courses.

Principle 1: *Know Your Learners*

Adult English learners are primed and ready to learn.

Prior to entering an academic subject course, adult English learners have probably spent one year to 18 months studying English, acquiring skills and strategies for success in their target EAP, EPP, or EOP programs. These learners have been explicitly taught strategies for reading effectively to grasp main ideas and details from text-based sources. They have learned strategies for note taking, written a multitude of essays, given single and group presentations, and participated in active learning classrooms. They have spent more time learning about learning than domestic students. (Banton, 2018)

- View adult English learners as a positive strength in classrooms. They bring world perspectives beyond those of native speakers and add value to the learning environment.
- Draw on these multiple perspectives to enrich learning for all course participants by giving adult English learners opportunities to share their experiences and perspectives.
- Learn the correct pronunciation of adult English learners' names and actively call on them by name.
- Conduct needs assessment at the beginning of the term to better know *who* learners are and not just *what* they know. Ask them a little bit about themselves, where they are from, and their perceptions on topics related to the host country.

Problem: Many international English learners do not understand the concept of "office hours." They may also be more hesitant to visit a professor due to cultural backgrounds and norms. One way for faculty to break the ice is to show that they are approachable. They can do this by showing up to class early and lingering afterward, reaching out to learners who are quiet in class, and trying to get everyone involved by paying attention to them.

- Consider learners' cultural backgrounds in lesson planning. Examples, idioms, and anecdotes that are included in a lesson may seem like common sense, but for an adult learner they can require extra effort to understand and may be alienating.
- Be mindful of the use of personal space and the gestures when interacting with adult learners from different cultures.
- Pay attention to academic and non-academic issues in learners' lives and reach out to high risk learners before high-stakes assessments to provide assistance and support. The chances are that these learners will be reluctant to initiate such contact.
- Be friendly—say hello, goodbye, and thank you. Kindness counts (Heng, 2017).

Principle 2: *Create Conditions for Language Learning*

- Review the course syllabus with your class. The syllabus should be as explicit as possible, listing all pertinent details related to the learning objectives, content topics, evaluation, important deadlines, and support options. During the term, refer back to the course outline so that learners understand the purpose of this document and rely on the information you provide to guide their studies.

7 Steps to Creating a Course Syllabus to Enhance Learning for Adult English learners

1. Provide all key information in written form for learners to refer to throughout the duration of the course.
2. Explain the importance of office hours and when and why to attend.
3. Provide detailed explanations of expectations for performance in class. If participation is evaluated, spell out expectations for exemplary practices.
4. Include assessment tools such as descriptive rubrics. Explain the purpose of assessment rubrics and how they are used to measure performance. Refer to the assessment rubrics before assignment deadlines to guide learner achievement.
5. Take the time to explain cultural and classroom norms or behaviours, as these may differ from learners' own cultural practices.
6. Explain the school's academic integrity policy related to academic issues such as plagiarism.
7. Become aware of the services available to learners on campus and provide links and contact information for support offices where learners can seek additional help, such as tutoring or mentoring services.

- Unpack target-culture idioms, anecdotes, and references in lectures, textbooks, and in-class discussions to assist learners in understanding materials. Adult learners may come from a variety of cultural backgrounds. Predict problematic areas ahead of time and prepare additional material or activities that will support understanding.
- Take an international approach to developing courses by including intercultural dimensions in the content of the curriculum. Provide opportunities for adult English learners to share examples, opinions, and cases from their cultures with their classmates. Create a global classroom where all learners contribute meaningfully and benefit (Leask, 2015).
- Make learning accessible with multi-modalities. Flipped and blended learning give adult English learners both time and a safe space to prepare for in-class work (Chapter 2, Practice 2.b). Post online chats and forums on the course management system to give these learners opportunities to engage and exchange with their peers that allow more time to understand, reflect, and respond.
- Create new learning situations that draw on the diverse backgrounds in the classroom so that all can learn with and from each other. This will engage learners in the learning process within and outside of the classroom (Leask & Carroll, 2011).
- Give learners time to learn the ropes by providing them an opportunity to submit drafts of their assignments and receive formative feedback.
- Empower learners to guide their own learning by giving them their choice in assignments.
- Avoid putting adult English learners on the spot to answer questions in class, as they may require time to formulate an answer and contribute meaningfully. Think-pair-share gives these learners an opportunity to test out what they want to communicate before speaking to the whole class.
- Employ active listening strategies and gestures when communicating with learners. Use reformulations and gestures such as nodding to demonstrate you understand what they are communicating.

Principle 3: *Design High-Quality Lessons for Language Development*

- Develop an awareness of the audience and design lessons accordingly.
- Help adult English learners learn the rhetoric. Define abbreviations and new terminology clearly. Expand on specific cultural references to facilitate comprehension and participation.
- Provide pre- and post-class tasks by referring to assigned course materials on the course management system to support learners' understanding and promote more active learning.
- Provide models of formal assignments that surpass, meet, and do not meet expectations to provide benchmarks for learners struggling with understanding expectations (Heng, 2017).
- Actively engage adult English learners by asking them their opinions on topics in class; this acknowledges their presence and makes them feel welcome.
- Adult learners from certain cultures may emphasize collective goals over individual ones in group work. When assigning group tasks, spell out expectations for individuals and the group as a whole, assign roles, and describe explicitly how participation and performance will be evaluated.

- Provide ways for learners to develop professional skills in addition to content knowledge and language proficiency. Integrate teamwork assignments and discuss the importance of working in teams and being an effective team member. In group work, assign small and large group work on structured and unstructured tasks for practice prior to high-stakes tasks (Volet & Ang, 1998).

Ella was in her first year at university when her professor assigned her first group project. She had spent nearly two years in an IEP prior to beginning her studies and had ample experience working in groups. Her professor assigned her to a group of four: three students from the host culture (all male) and Ella (female, adult English learner). When the groups broke out to discuss the task and to delegate work, the three male students excluded Ella. Ella left the class feeling frustrated, disrespected, and upset. Her first instinct was to drop the class, but instead she went to talk with the professor. The professor, who had been observing the groups as they conducted the initial breakout discussions, told Ella that she had noticed the group dynamic, asked Ella what role she thought she would like to play in the group, and encouraged Ella to ask for that role. In addition, when the class next met, the professor distributed a roles worksheet to each group, noting that part of each learner's grade would depend on both contributions to the group's work and intentional inclusion of all group members. The professor assigned the task of maintaining the roles worksheet to one learner in each group; in Ella's group, the professor assigned that task to Ella.

Principle 5: *Monitor and Assess Learner Language Development*

- Make feedback as accessible as possible. Communicate expectations with clarity and flexibility. Clarify the weighting of a grade in a rubric with descriptors of performance.
- Reach out to learners who are struggling following the first assignment and invite them to a one-on-one meeting to assess their situation and provide guidance for obtaining additional support.

Principle 6: *Engage and Collaborate Within a Community of Practice*

The Langdon Film School has a 50/50 ratio of adult English learners and domestic learners in its three-year program. The school favours hiring instructors with strong technical backgrounds in film production over experience in teaching. The pedagogical approach is predominantly lecture-based with an emphasis on project-based learning. With the influx of adult English learners in the program, the school has recognized the importance of drawing on the expertise of ESP teachers to assist the content teachers in teaching these learners effectively and developing a parallel English language program to support learners throughout their film studies.

- Draw on the expertise of ESL or EFL teachers and specialists on staff for support in teaching adult English learners (Harper & de Jong, 2009). For example, learn about effective ESL-related teaching strategies and techniques, such as scaffolding and simplifying content (review Table 3.1 for practices that provide and enhance input through varied techniques, approaches and modalities).
- Collaborate with ESL or EFL teachers and specialists on staff to design and develop adaptable tasks and projects.
- Learn about the school's resources to develop a full picture of the support available to adult English learners and other learners. Attend an academic orientation or meet with support service staff to prepare to inform adult English learners about the purpose of campus facilities and guide them in obtaining academic help, advising, and more.

Guidance and Learning Counselors

Cheng, a student from China, came to Canada to study business. Studying abroad was not his first choice as he would have rather studied with his high school friends, but the competition for a place at a top-notch university in China was out of the question for Cheng. Before coming to North America, he had hopes of becoming actively involved in university clubs much like he was in high school in Shanghai, but he worried about fitting in as he heard stories from his friends who were also studying in North America. Now in Canada, Cheng has insulated himself in "Chinaada" (living in a Chinese community in Canada). Cheng's girlfriend and roommate are also from China. As a part-time job, Cheng washes dishes in a popular Chinese restaurant. Cheng speaks English only when put on the spot in class and has little or no interaction with Canadians or other international students. Cheng just received his first term midterm grades and is failing three out of four classes. If his grades do not improve by the end of the term, he will be put on academic probation. How would you advise him? (Banton, 2018).

Adult English learners who choose to study or work abroad commonly experience language barriers, academic difficulties, financial difficulties, interpersonal problems with host peers, discrimination, loss of social support, homesickness, and alienation. Intentionally or unintentionally, they may find themselves in circumstances where they are alienated from their peers, such as Cheng in the above example. One of the greatest challenges for these adult learners is language difficulties, which may affect academic and psychological adjustment (Lin & Yi, 1997).

This section provides direction for academic guidance and learning counselors working with adult English learners. The challenges that these learners face go beyond English language learning and mean that a one-on-one relationship is essential for giving them the support they need to achieve their goals. Most of the actions outlined in this section refer to an EAP academic setting; however, some may also be applicable to EPP and EOP programs at universities or the professional workplace.

Principle 1: *Know Your Learners*

"In terms of student services, it's really about knowing your student body and offering them the things that they need. Our student body is primarily from the Middle East, and we are always looking for ways to connect with them and get them involved on campus. For example, we assisted students in organizing an Omani National Day on campus. The students reserved a space on the main walk of campus, handed out Omani flags, and had stations with traditional food, tea, and henna. By sharing their culture, our students can better integrate into the campus community."
—Alyssa Swanson, IEP Manager, Penn.

- Get to the core of the issue by speaking directly with adult English learners. Treat each learner as an individual who experiences unique challenges and problems.
- Provide information on different services at orientations and follow up with reminders to encourage learners use these services.
- Adult English learners often experience culture shock, homesickness, or reality shock, and may have negative perceptions of mental health services. If warranted, recommend they visit these services and help them make appointments and/or accompany them.
- Help adult English learners learn how to advocate for themselves and obtain the support they need by encouraging them to use available resources to address the challenges they are experiencing.

Principle 2: *Create Conditions for Language Learning*

- Encourage adult English learners to seek out opportunities to get involved in their new communities and develop relationships with other international and domestic students. Give them strategies and point out opportunities for networking on campus.
- Encourage adult English learners to live the language and cultural experience by participating in campus activities through their departments, student organizations and clubs, and international student offices.
- If a student mentor program exists at your school, try to match the adult learner with a native speaker or an experienced international student.
- Empower adult English learners by having them mentor native speakers going abroad through a cultural exchange program.
- Encourage English adult learners to subscribe to social media sites in English to stay abreast of current events and activities. This type of information not only helps them feel more connected, but also fosters more conversation with native-speaking peers.
- Encourage adult learners to organize social events and invite peers from different cultures to encourage speaking English as a common language.
- Suggest that adult English learners volunteer at offices that require them to speak English.
- Develop programs that build community and connections for adult English learners. For example, invite them to conversation groups that will help them improve their English conversation skills. Select conversation topics that are related to learners' personal interests, such dressing for North American winter and strategies in making friends. Invite experts from relevant professional fields to join for a session.
- Guide adult English learners to training and resources such as computer skills, library services, and writing centers to foster their English language development and their success as learners across different academic disciplines.
- When advising on academic skills, help learners
  - Develop active note-taking, active reading, and previewing texts for reading, active listening, and writing skills.
  - Focus on higher order concerns first. In writing, for example, begin with organization and meaning, then other concerns such as grammar and sentence structure.
  - "Notice" their recurring errors and understand how to correct them.
  - Understand their professors' expectations by breaking down assignments, rubrics, and expectations.

In a medical residency program at a U.S. university, residency supervisors identified issues that adult English learner residents were experiencing related to understanding cultural norms that differed from those of their home countries. They held certain biases towards alcohol consumption, which affected their neutrality in interviewing patients. In their countries, alcohol is forbidden, and the residents were not aware that in most cases alcohol is consumed in moderation in the United States. Working with guidance counselors on campus, the supervisors developed a three-step program for international medical graduates in residency that consisted of a cultural orientation and lecture series to better sensitize them to U.S. cultural norms.

Principle 6: *Engage and Collaborate Within a Community of Practice*

- Advocate on behalf of adult English learners by voicing their concerns to program and school administrators. Guidance and learning counselors can bring adult learners' issues to light, spurring improvements to services and programs at their institutions.

A Look Back and a Look Ahead

Chapter 4 has examined the roles of a range of institution-based professionals whose work complements that of ESP teaching staff in supporting the education of adult English learners. For each group of practitioners, the chapter has outlined key actions and offered helpful resources to aid in the full implementation of The 6 Principles for Exemplary Teaching of English Learners. In making these recommendations, the chapter has highlighted the following ideas, based on research and best practice:

- Successful programs depend on establishing a strong culture of shared responsibility for adult English learners across all stakeholders at an institution.
- Adult English learners bring linguistic and cultural resources to institutions, programs, and classrooms. These assets should be welcomed, promoted, and fully used to strengthen teaching and learning. This can be accomplished by taking time to investigate the linguistic and cultural resources that adult English learners possess.
- Equity and access can be achieved only if all professionals work together to ensure that adult English learners receive high-quality programs and services designed to support their educational success in a positive, welcoming climate.
- All personnel can aid in the delivery of high-quality lessons for language and content development, adapting instruction as needed for key learner characteristics. They can also assist in monitoring and assessing learners' language development and academic achievement in ways that are culturally and linguistically appropriate, valid, and fair.
- Institutional leaders, program administrators, non-ESL faculty, and guidance and academic counselors can ensure the success of adult English learners when they consider these learners' educational needs carefully and act on them.

This chapter focused on institution-based professionals as key educators who are most able to implement The 6 Principles, but they are not alone. Many other professionals are involved in the education of adult learners, including state policymakers and curriculum and test developers, who, despite their distance from the classroom, affect the education of all learners. Test developers and curriculum writers in particular have a direct impact on learners; they can either support or frustrate the success of adult learners by the ways in which their products are designed and implemented or interpreted. Indeed, all the professionals named here can benefit by reviewing The 6 Principles so that they can honor them as they fulfill their important roles.

Chapter 5 builds on the practices described in this book and demonstrates The 6 Principles in action in five distinct ESP contexts. It maps out the principles and illustrates the effective practices of successful teachers as they adapt the principles to their contexts to serve the needs of their learners.

Additional resources for this book are available at www.the6principles.org/eap-esp.

5 THE 6 PRINCIPLES IN DIFFERENT PROGRAM CONTEXTS

The 6 Principles for Exemplary Teaching of English Learners are relevant to all kinds of teaching programs. It is important, however, that teachers think about the underlying ideas and adapt the practices according to their own teaching context. This means that different elements in the framework will be given different emphases, depending on the situation. The aim of this chapter is to describe five ESP classes operating in very different contexts to demonstrate how instructors use The 6 Principles to provide exemplary teaching.

The cases described in this chapter are based on real programs, although names, locations, and some details have been changed for anonymity. Read through the five cases to see how The 6 Principles can be adapted to suit different contexts and to consider how they might be implemented in other teaching situations.

The five cases are as follows:

- A preparation course for learners needing to pass the TOEFL iBT® test as part of the admission procedure for university study in the United States
- An academic writing course at a German university
- A large MBA class in India
- Sales engineers in Mexico preparing to negotiate with international business partners
- Caregivers in Indonesia improving their English to better interact with patients overseas

Passing the TOEFL iBT Test

The TOEFL iBT test is accepted by higher education institutions all over the world. According to the Educational Testing Service (ETS) website, the "TOEFL iBT test measures your ability to use and understand English at the university level. And it evaluates how well you combine your reading, listening, speaking and writing skills to perform academic tasks" (ETS, n.d.).

Marjorie teaches in a TOEFL iBT intensive English program (IEP) in a language school in the United States. The course is one module of a much longer program designed to help adult learners apply for undergraduate studies at an American university. The class consists of adult learners from all over the world. Some have already attempted the test but have not yet been successful. They are aged between 17 and 23 and need to get a minimum score of 90 on the TOEFL iBT in order to gain admission. The learners attend five hours of class each day from Monday to Friday for two weeks, for a total of 50 hours, and are expected to spend the rest of the time on preparation, review of materials, and assignments. There is also a scheduled one-to-one session with the teacher every week, where individual needs are discussed and feedback is given.

For the learners this is very much a high stakes test—they must get a high score on the test in order to achieve their aims. They or their families have also invested a considerable amount of money in travel, accommodation, and course fees. The advantage is that the IEP has a good reputation and a good record of success; and because the school has an entry requirement of CEFR C1, most learners pass the TOEFL iBT with flying colors.

Common European Framework of Reference (CEFR) C1 Global Scale:

Can understand a wide range of demanding, longer texts, and recognize implicit meaning. Can express him/herself fluently and spontaneously without much obvious searching for expressions. Can use language flexibly and effectively for social, academic and occupational purposes. Can produce clear, well-structured, detailed text on complex subjects, showing controlled use of organizational patterns, connectors and cohesive devices.

Source: https://rm.coe.int/1680459f97

The TOEFL iBT test covers four language skills—reading, listening, speaking, and writing—and there is no pass or fail. Test takers receive a score, and each institution sets its own requirements for admission purposes. What is certain is that each learner will need to get a high score in all four skills. The following samples of high score performance descriptions which might appear on test-taker score reports give an idea of what is expected.

Reading

Test takers who receive a score at the HIGH level typically understand academic texts in English that require a wide range of reading abilities regardless of the difficulty of the texts. Test takers who score at the HIGH level typically:

- have a very good command of academic vocabulary and grammatical structure
- can understand and connect information, make appropriate inferences, and synthesize ideas, even when the text is conceptually dense, and the language is complex
- can recognize the expository organization of a text and the role that specific information serves within the larger text, even when the text is conceptually dense
- can abstract major ideas from a text, even when the text is conceptually dense and contains complex language

Listening

Test takers who receive a score at the HIGH level typically understand conversations and lectures in English that present a wide range of listening demands. These demands can include difficult vocabulary (uncommon terms, or colloquial or figurative language), complex grammatical structures, abstract or complex ideas, and/or making sense of unexpected or seemingly contradictory information. When listening to lectures and conversations like these, test takers at the HIGH level typically can:

- understand main ideas and important details, whether they are stated or implied
- distinguish more important ideas from less important ones
- understand how information is being used (for example, to provide evidence for a claim or describe a step in a complex process)
- recognize how pieces of information are connected (for example, in a cause-and-effect relationship)
- understand many different ways that speakers use language for purposes other than to give information (for example, to emphasize a point, express agreement or disagreement, or convey intentions indirectly)
- synthesize information, even when it is not presented in sequence, and make correct inferences on the basis of that information

Speaking about familiar topics

Your responses indicate an ability to communicate your personal experiences and opinions effectively in English. Overall, your speech is clear and fluent. Your use of vocabulary and grammar is effective with only minor errors. Your ideas are generally well developed and expressed coherently

Speaking about campus situations

Your responses indicate an ability to speak effectively in English about reading material and conversations typically encountered by university learners. Overall, your responses are clear and coherent, with only occasional errors of pronunciation, grammar or vocabulary

Speaking about academic course content

Your responses demonstrate an ability to communicate effectively in English about academic topics typical of first-year university studies. Your speech is mostly clear and fluent. You are able to use appropriate vocabulary and grammar to explain concepts and ideas from reading or lecture material. You are able to talk about key information and relevant details with only minor inaccuracies.

Writing based on reading and listening

You responded well to the task, relating the lecture to the reading. Weaknesses, if you have any, might have to do with:

- slight imprecision in your summary of some of the main points
- use of English that is occasionally ungrammatical or unclear

Writing based on knowledge and experience

You responded with a well-organized and developed essay. Weaknesses, if you have any, might have to do with:

- use of English that is occasionally ungrammatical, unclear or unidiomatic
- elaboration of ideas or connection of ideas that could have been stronger

(Source: adapted from https://www.ets.org/Media/Tests/TOEFL/pdf/TOEFL_Perf_Feedpdf)

It is a while since Marjorie has run a TOEFL preparation class. She has heard that the test has recently been redesigned, and one of her initial tasks will be to make sure she fully understands the new format.

Principle 1. *Know Your Learners*

The learners in the class come from a wide variety of countries in Europe, Asia, and Africa. They have all completed questionnaires and a placement test, and Marjorie has detailed information about their other languages, education, hobbies and interests, and course goals. All are experienced language learners, and most have already taken standardized language proficiency tests in their own countries. Although they have all graduated from high school in their own countries, have the necessary qualifications (other than English) to enter their chosen universities, and have similar goals, they do not share the same educational backgrounds and experiences, so their means of achieving their goals might vary. Most importantly, their attitudes toward education and the role of the teacher differ widely. Some expect the teacher to give them all the guidance they need, but they also expect to have to work hard outside class to achieve their goals. Others see the teacher as being paid to do a job, in this case get them through the test, and they see the responsibility for this as being largely in the teacher's hands. These different attitudes are influenced by the learners' own personalities and learning experiences, and Marjorie will need to keep these attitudes in mind as she runs the course.

None of the learners have ever lived in the United States, and the class is as much an introduction to American ways of education as it is a language preparation class. From years of experience working in different countries, Marjorie is fully aware that the American way of doing things is not necessarily the only way of doing things, and she knows that what some will take for granted may cause unexpected challenges for others. Another issue for a few of the learners is their struggle to understand some of the accents they are encountering in the school environment.

Nevertheless, the overall mood of the class is good. The learners are motivated and eager to learn, excited about the new situation they find themselves in, and willing to make friends and help each other. Marjorie starts the class with Getting to Know You activities that allow the learners not only to get to know her, but also each other.

Principle 2. *Create Conditions for Language Learning*

Marjorie is very conscious that the learners in this class are depending on her to help them pass the TOEFL iBT and meet the entrance level requirements for their admission to study at the university. She does not have a lot of time, and she must prioritize what will help them the most.

She is also aware that, although the placement tests suggest that their English is good enough to pass the test, such tests do not always correlate with actual results. Other issues can come into the equation, such as homesickness and stress. Her aim is to build trust and a personal relationship with each learner in the short time she has with them. To do this, she talks to individuals informally during activities and class breaks and makes sure they know they can confide in her with any issues if they so wish, and that she will do her best to help. In a way, her style is very similar to that of a sports coach—everyone on the team has the ability to perform to the required standard, and her role is to make individual learners confident about success. For example, one learner tells Marjorie that she is feeling left out—she has not met anyone else from her country, and all the other learners seem to have found friends. Marjorie is able to put her in touch with a learner from another class, which seems to alleviate the problem.

Principle 3. *Design High-Quality Lessons for Language Development*

Marjorie knows that one of the key issues for passing the TOEFL test is knowing the format and style of the questions, and preparing thoroughly for each section. Luckily, there is plenty of test preparation material available, which allows her to replicate the test tasks, and she uses this material as a basis for the teaching. In the first week, she focuses on one test section per day, analyzing it carefully with the learners and making sure that everybody understands exactly what is required.

TOEFL iBT Test Section	
Reading	3–4 reading passages 10 questions each 54–72 minutes
Listening	3–4 lectures, 6 questions each 2–3 conversations, 5 questions each 41–57 minutes
Speaking	4 tasks 1 independent 3 integrated 17 minutes
Writing	2 tasks 50 minutes

(Source: https://www.ets.org/toefl/better_test_experience)

A Day in Marjorie's TOEFL Prep Class

Marjorie has five hours with the class each day, which she divides into three sections, each of one and a half hours, and two 15-minute breaks.

She begins her day with a game to warm the class up and inject a bit of energy into the room. The class has asked for activities which recycle language already covered, and today learners work in pairs to complete a crossword puzzle, focusing on words they are likely to meet in the test. Clues are at different ends of the room, so learners move around in order to find their clues. The first pair to complete the puzzle wins a small prize, so there is plenty of enthusiasm and the activity is quite loud. Marjorie checks answers as a whole-class activity, which lets her monitor understanding and clarify any language issues, before informing the class who has won.

Once the excitement has died down, Marjorie starts the next stage of the lesson, which involves an introduction to a specific section of the test. Today the focus is on the listening section, and the class watches a short video that explains the format and types of questions. In a class discussion after the video, she answers questions as necessary and asks a few questions of her own to check that everyone is clear about the format.

After a 15-minute break, Marjorie starts the second one-and-a-half-hour section by giving the learners the chance to try out some typical listening section tasks. These involve listening to a short excerpt from a lecture or conversation, and then answering a series of multiple-choice questions about what they have just heard. She plays the recordings, allowing learners to take notes, just as they would in the real test. The learners then choose their answers, after which she shares the solutions and discusses each question in turn. She then repeats the procedure two more times, each time with a different text and a different set of questions.

After the second 15-minute break, Marjorie starts the third section. She asks learners to form small groups, discuss what they found easy or difficult about the tasks, and brainstorm possible strategies for improving their scores. The groups then share their ideas with the rest of the class. Marjorie adds comments and provides additional feedback based on her own observations and experience. She informs the learners that there are many more examples of listening section tasks in the course materials, makes sure that all the learners know where to find them, and

(continued)

(continued)

suggests that they do more practice on this section after class. Since they all need to get a specific score to gain admission to their chosen universities, she reminds them that this is the time to really work on any weaknesses they may feel they have.

The last 15 minutes of the section is for quiet time and reflection. Learners go through their notes from the morning's work and think about what they have learned. Individually they also work out their learning plan for the rest of the day, write it on a piece of paper, and give it to Marjorie as they leave the class.

Principle 4. *Adapt Lesson Delivery as Needed*

Although the day's overall routine is the same, the demands of each section of the test, as well as learners' own reactions and feedback, require Marjorie to think on her feet and adapt where necessary. Formative assessment, which allows her to check learner performance on individual tasks, helps with this. Some tasks are easier than others, and she realizes that she does not have to spend as much time on them. Likewise, as she gets to know the class and their individual needs and possible weaknesses, she plans a differentiated approach to allow learners to do different tasks in their own time. She groups learners according to needs, with each group targeting different aspects of the test. So, one group focuses more on writing skills, one on speaking, and so on. Here she guides learners to extra practice activities so that they can address the areas they need. Sometimes she is able to send the groups to empty classrooms so that they can discuss issues without disturbing the others in the class.

Principle 5. *Monitor and Assess Learner Language Development*

Marjorie's overall design of the course means that there are regular chances to see the learners working on the various test types. Sometimes she gives feedback to the group as a whole, and sometimes she finds time to give individual feedback when she is alone with a learner. Confidence building is a key factor here, and she makes sure that she praises good performance as much as possible. She also makes sure that she reminds learners to monitor their own performances and record areas that need to be improved. This practice, combined with her requirement for each learner to give her a note after each class telling her what their afternoon's learning plan is, gives her useful insights she might otherwise have missed.

Principle 6. *Engage and Collaborate Within a Community of Practice*

Marjorie is lucky enough to be working in an IEP that specializes in TOEFL prep, and there are other teachers who run similar classes. Every day after class, they meet informally in the teachers' room to discuss ideas and compare notes. Marjorie takes this opportunity to ask advice on various issues and problems when they arise. Sometimes the school director of studies is available and joins in the discussions. These informal meetings are very important in making sure that everyone on the team is up to date on the latest changes to the test requirements, availability of new publications and online resources, research on teaching strategies, and so on. The teachers respect and trust each other, and the system works well.

An Academic Writing Course at a German University

Christian teaches in the English language training (ELT) department in a large German university. Undergraduates in Germany typically do their writing in German, but students in graduate school are often required to write their papers in English. To help them, the university offers optional (non-credit) 15-week academic writing courses. The course comes with a set of materials, which the university has developed and which Christian has used in the past. He knows that he will not be able to cover all the materials in the time he has available (90 minutes per week for 15 weeks), so he will have to choose according to his learners' needs.

Principle 1. *Know Your Learners*
All the learners have passed IELTS or TOEFL at a high level (IELTS Band 6.5 and TOEFL 90), so he knows they are all capable of handling the course. However, this will be the first time that many of them will be focusing on academic English writing in such detail, and this will certainly be challenging for some. As he knows from his own experience, some learners may be proficient readers of academic texts, but most will find writing them another matter. As always, the class is international, and has 22 learners from a range of different linguistic and cultural backgrounds. Christian has worked with such classes many times, but this year there is a difference: the class includes a group of refugees who have recently arrived in Germany. Like all students at the university, they had to have the correct academic credentials in order to gain admission, but he is concerned that some unexpected issues may arise.

Due to the large influx of refugees in recent years, the German government has created several support centers for refugees that give help as necessary. The university also offers academic support in its students' service center. Christian has decided to attend a refugee awareness workshop, which is designed to help Germans understand more about refugees and their unique situations. One result of this workshop is that he makes a conscious effort to allow himself extra time to get to know the refugees in the class.

Principle 2. *Create Conditions for Language Learning*
The students in the class are all experienced learners, but Christian feels there is a lot he can do to make the learning more successful. Part of this involves making them feel comfortable with each other, so he decides to use the first session for everyone in the class to get to know each other. To make sure that the refugees meet their new classmates, he uses random grouping techniques, so they do not always gravitate to their own sub-group.

He also decides to negotiate the syllabus, fully aware that the technique might be new to some learners, but knowing that it will give him a good idea of what individuals want from the course. At the same time, the process demonstrates that the course is inevitably a compromise with so many learners in it. From experience he knows that the main advantage of a negotiated syllabus is that when the learners invest time and effort in deciding the syllabus themselves, and therefore in a sense own the course, they will be much more committed.

Christian uses a questionnaire (see Figure 5.1) and the university materials as resources. After the class has spent 45 minutes getting to know each other, he explains that the university materials are too lengthy and that the class will need to decide which topics to include and which to exclude. First he takes the class through a typical unit, showing how it is divided into four parts (Speaking, Reading, Writing, and Listening). He points out that since the course is aimed at academic writing, he feels that only the Writing sections need to be looked at. He then asks the learners, first individually, and next in pairs to agree on which specific writing topics in the materials will be most useful. He then has a whole-class discussion where each pair shares its choices with the rest of the class, and finally they generate an agreed syllabus that everyone accepts. He emphasizes that these choices provide work for the next 12 weeks, and that the final two weeks will be devoted to personal choice. He explains that the class can decide to re-negotiate at any time.

Negotiating the syllabus

The table below shows a list of sections that we could cover on the course. However, time is limited, and we need to decide which sections will be most useful. Please go through the book and identify <u>eight</u> sections you would most like to work through. Mark these in Column 2 (My choice). Then find a partner and compare your choices. Agree on <u>ten</u> sections together and mark your choices in Column 3 (Pair choice). As a class, we will then decide which <u>twelve</u> sections we would most like to study.

FIGURE 5.1 Syllabus Questionnaire

Writing topics	My choice (max 8)	Pair choice (max 10)	Class choice (max 12)
Types of articles			
Writing as process			
Writing as product			
Writing abstracts			
Writing introductions			
Literature reviews			
Discussing findings			
Problems and solutions			
Explaining cause and effect			
Argument and counterargument			
Making comparisons			
Using visual information			
Writing conclusions			
References and citations			
Vocabulary—collocations			
Vocabulary—prefixes and suffixes			
Vocabulary—nouns and adjectives			
Vocabulary—verbs and adverbs			
Vocabulary—hedging language			
Grammar—punctuation			
Grammar—relative clauses			
Grammar—modals			

Principle 3. Design High-Quality Lessons for Language Development
Christian fully understands the importance of setting objectives for each lesson, and here he uses the university materials as his main resource. Each unit has clear objectives, which the class has already agreed to. However, he also understands that learners will benefit from bringing their own language experience into their learning, and so he encourages the students to compare the materials and examples in this class's materials with what they encounter in their own research and in other classes in the university. For example, he uses the material on collocations to introduce the concept and get the learners thinking about the usefulness of noun phrases, and then asks them to find examples from texts relevant to their own subject area. The law students in the class find examples like *previous legislation* and *maximum benefits*, the business studies group finds *fixed rate of interest* and *economic policy*, and the engineering learners find *automotive industry* and *produce heat*. Likewise, when the class works on the citations and referencing section, he asks learners to find examples in their own texts of the reporting verbs (e.g., say, talk about, think, emphasize, show, and suggest) discussed in the course book.

A lesson in an academic English writing class

The lesson is supposed to last 90 minutes, but the culture in the university means that some learners arrive up to a quarter of an hour late. Christian uses this time to chat with those learners who arrive earlier, making small talk but also informally assessing how their studies are progressing. Once everyone is seated, the lesson can begin.

Today the topic is Writing Introductions. Christian starts by asking the learners to brainstorm the features learners might expect to find in a typical opening paragraph. He then asks the class to do the first task in the materials, which requires them to read an introduction and identify specific features. This takes 10 minutes, and he asks learners to share their answers with the person sitting next to them. After some further discussion as a group, the class works through additional tasks. Learners move at different speeds through the tasks, as always, and Christian spends his time walking around the classroom, quietly checking learners' progress, making suggestions and answering questions where necessary. Sometimes learners ask questions that Christian feels will be relevant to the whole class, and he keeps his answers very brief, telling the learner that he will discuss this later. He calls a halt once he is satisfied that everyone in the room has done at least the first two exercises. He then leads the class through the two exercises, asking learners to give their answers, reacting to learners' comments and queries, and giving feedback. He then asks learners to look at texts from their own disciplines, and compare those opening paragraphs with the work they have just done.

He ends the class by asking learners to record a key point they have learned. As several report out, he summarizes the key points which come up, and adds others. He reminds the learners that they should keep their eyes open for sample thesis statements as they read in their own subject areas.

Principle 4. *Adapt Lesson Delivery as Needed*
One of the main issues Christian must deal with is the fact that his learners come from different academic disciplines, and many of the examples in the course book seem irrelevant to the learners at times. In order to make the materials more engaging, he often divides the class into groups representing various disciplines in the class (as in the collocations example above). While this is clearly a compromise, he finds that the learners are thus able to share examples and discuss issues that are far more personally relevant.

Another challenge Christian must deal with is seating arrangements. Normally, the room is set up with seats and tables clustered in small groups, ideal for small group work, but occasionally he is required to teach his class in a lecture hall, where the seating is fixed in tiered rows. With no space to walk around, it is hard for him to check on progress and learners can only do individual or pair work. These lessons tend to be much more teacher-centered, which is not ideal, but he realizes he must work with the situation he has.

Principle 5. *Monitor and Assess Learner Language Development*

Christian finishes each class with a short period of reflection and encourages his learners to have a look at the section objectives and judge if they have been met on a scale of one to five. Christian keeps short notes on each learner, including this self-assessment grade, as well as possible difficulties. Sometimes he makes these notes during the class, but more often he makes them at the end. It is difficult to make real judgments about everybody in the group as it is so large, but he does his best.

He also tries to talk to learners for a few minutes after class and gauge their reaction to the activities as well as how they feel they are doing. However, normally the learners are in a rush to get to their next class, and he knows there are several learners he has never spoken to directly. He does, however, make sure that he speaks with each refugee as often as possible because he is aware that their circumstances are more challenging than those of the German students in his class. Acclimating to a new learning environment and experiencing the double challenge of acquiring German and English simultaneously is arduous for the refugee learners. He regularly invites them to office hours to help them and discuss their academic progress and to reiterate that campus support services are available should they require additional support.

Christian's other main monitoring tool is asking for samples of learners' work. All the sections in the materials offer several different activities, and he asks learners to send him one task by email each week. Unfortunately, his schedule does not allow more, and some learners forget, but at least he gets a glimpse into what the learners are producing and where possible problem areas might be.

Principle 6. *Engage and Collaborate Within a Community of Practice*

Christian has regular contact with other English language teachers. He is a member of a local teachers' association which holds regular workshops and social get-togethers, and although few of the teachers he meets work at a university, he really enjoys the chance to share his experiences and listen to what others have to say. What he finds most enjoyable is the fact that these teachers are almost all freelance and come from all over the world. Some are very experienced, while others are only planning to teach English for a few years. They all have different perspectives. In this community, many of his peers are also teaching learners with similar demographic backgrounds, which Christian finds helpful so he can better understand and support the realities of his learners.

A Large MBA Business English Class in India

Rahul works in a university in New Delhi. The university has been running a Master's of Business Administration (MBA) program for some years, and Rahul has considerable experience in this regard. In addition to a master's degree in TESOL, he has an MBA. The learners typically have undergraduate degrees in areas such as engineering, finance, and IT, as well as a minimum of five years' experience in the workplace. Some have considerably more than this. Most, but not all, are Indian nationals. As part of the program prerequisites, the minimum level is IELTS Band 7 or

TOEFL 94. Because all the teaching is in English, the program includes remedial business English classes for those who request it. These classes are designed to provide support in the types of language and skills the learners encounter in the MBA program. Classes are 90 minutes long and take place once a week for the duration of the semester. The class size is large; attendance tends to be between 70 and 80 participants per class.

The curriculum is based on case studies, which are common in business English classes all over the world. There are good reasons for this. A typical case study consists of input information, which gives the background and context, and a business problem, which needs to be solved. Learners are themselves—there is no role playing—and the output requires learners to use business communication skills, such as summarizing the discussion via minutes, emails, or a presentation. The final activity is a conversation where learners analyze each other's approaches to the problem and provide feedback and comments. As such, the communication skills required hew closely to those used in the real world of business. The classes not only provide plenty of practice and exposure to real business language, but they do so in the context of other transferable skills such as critical thinking, teamwork, communication skills, and collaboration.

It is worth noting that the case studies used in these classes are different from the case studies used in other parts of the MBA program, which are typically much more detailed and require other specific business skills (e.g., accounting and financial analysis). Those teachers have more time available; Rahul has only 90 minutes per case study. Rahul may also simplify the language in the cases, depending on the English proficiency of the learners.

The teacher's role is twofold: first, to prepare the case study, normally in collaboration with a subject specialist, who makes sure that the content is closely related to the MBA studies, and second, to run the case study, observe the learners closely, identify issues and assist as necessary, and then provide language feedback and appropriate learning activities to improve the language competence. The methodology fits squarely into the communicative language teaching/task-based teaching approach—the learners are primarily using the language to solve a problem, and the task requires them not only to understand written and spoken input, but also to collaborate with other learners in order to discuss the issues.

This semester the class is focused on human resources (HR) management, so the case studies are in this area.

Stages

1. Reading input documents
2. Defining the issue or problem
3. Identifying options
4. Selecting best option and presenting the solution
5. Evaluating the solution
6. Task feedback
7. Language feedback
8. Optional follow-up language work

Principle 1. *Know Your Learners*

As someone who has been through a similar MBA course himself, Rahul is very aware of the pressures the learners are under. With only 90 minutes a week, and with such a large number of learners, he does not have a lot of time to get to know his learners as well as he would like, but he tries his best before the class starts by circulating an online survey. He also does his best to interact with them individually during the class, but this is difficult with such large numbers.

Although the learners have all reached the admission level of English, the wide variety of accents and cultures in the classroom can be challenging for some learners. The Indians have no problem understanding each other, but the learners from other countries have more difficulty with the Indian accent. Rahul makes a point of mentioning this issue to the Indian students, and finds he must continually remind them that intelligibility is a key part of successful communication.

Principle 2. *Create Conditions for Language Learning*

The learners are highly motivated and fully aware that English language skills are vital for their success. However, they also appreciate the more relaxed atmosphere in the English classes, where the successful outcome of the case study is not so critical to their final grade. Rahul sees his main task as making sure that learners develop the skills and strategies for thinking carefully about the language they encounter and the language they use. He has spent some time explaining the concept of "noticing," which he feels is a useful strategy for his learners to develop. Keenly aware that accents can be challenging for some learners, he tries to make sure that the learners ask for clarification when necessary. As this is a vital skill in international business, he feels that the skills the learners develop in this regard will stand them in good stead.

Principle 3. *Design High-Quality Lessons for Language Development*

The case study method is a familiar methodology in an MBA course and is well understood by the learners. They enjoy the challenge of understanding the issues and exploring ways to solve the problem, and they also appreciate the chance to give their own opinions. Given the limited amount of class time, Rahul gives out the advance reading material a week before the class and expects learners to arrive having read the context of the case.

From a language teaching perspective, there are certain strategies Rahul does to help his learners with their language development.

- First, learners do not all receive the same advance reading materials, which means that there is an information gap and learners are required to communicate with each other to get access to the information they need. Rahul circulates during this time and makes sure that everyone fully understands the situation.
- Second, he encourages learners to ask him questions about the language they have come across, and if he feels it necessary, he pre-teaches some key vocabulary. To help him make this decision, he runs his texts through an online vocabulary profiler, which groups words according to level. Although he is aware that there are many ways to pre-teach vocabulary, shortage of time and the size of the class mean that he generally highlights the words and provides definitions and examples of the words in sample sentences.
- Third, depending on the case, he may also cover communication skills, such as managing meetings or giving presentations, although there is not a lot of time for this.
- Finally, he mixes the groups so that learners regularly work with different partners. Although the basic teaching strategy is the same with each case study, he finds that each one presents its own challenges and requires him to be flexible.

A typical 120-minute case study lesson

Rahul starts the session by welcoming everybody to the class and asks specific questions to check that they have all read the advance materials. Using the jigsaw technique, he divides the class into small groups, making sure that each group includes learners who have read the different documents. This week the case study is about choosing a new production engineer for a fictitious company, and the advance materials include résumés from the different candidates, as well as background information on the company and the job description of the position. The task for the learners is to provide a short list of three candidates who will be invited forward for interviews. He allows 15 minutes for the learners to brief each other on the information they have, and then discuss and clarify any outstanding issues. Each group also has a designated note taker who does not take part in the case study discussions. The note taker's job is to observe the interactions and record any miscommunication issues that arise. For example, the note taker may observe that someone asked for clarification, but it was never given, or may note that the clarification was inaccurate and make suggestions for improvement.

Once the groups are satisfied with the discussion, they move to the next stage—listing the advantages and disadvantages of each candidate. Forty-five minutes before the end of the lesson, Rahul stops the discussion and asks the groups to make their final decision. As no candidate meets all the criteria, there is plenty of additional discussion before the groups makes their final short lists. Rahul allows a further 10 minutes for this, and then again asks each group to make their final decision, which he writes the board. This inevitably causes additional discussion as the groups compare their lists. Finally, Rahul asks each learner to write an email to the HR manager giving the reasons for their top three choices and asks that these are sent to him in the next 20 minutes. The class goes quiet and everyone is fully concentrated on the task. They know that Rahul will send them feedback on the quality of their email.

Every class ends with a 10-minute feedback session, and this class is no exception. Rahul keeps this simple and asks the learners to comment briefly on three things: what they liked about the case study, what they didn't like, and what they might change. He also uses this time to address any language issues that may have arisen. When the time is up, the learners leave the room, still discussing the results of the case study. Rahul knows it was a good lesson.

Class outline (total 120 minutes):
Welcome and check that advance materials have been read (5 minutes)
Divide class into groups (5 minutes)
Group sharing of information (15 minutes)
Groups list advantages and disadvantages (50 minutes)
Final group discussion (10 minutes)
Class discussion (5 minutes)
Email writing (20 minutes)
Feedback session (10 minutes)

Principle 4. *Adapt Lesson Delivery as Needed*

Although each class follows a similar format, each case study and ensuing discussion are different. Rahul often finds it challenging to keep within a 120-minute lesson plan, particularly as he is loath to break up good discussions, and sometimes he does not manage to leave enough time for one of the tasks or the final feedback activity. In these cases, he sends everyone in the class a short text message asking for their comments, which he usually receives quickly. The use of technology is one key way he manages the large class size.

Principle 5. *Monitor and Assess Learner Language Development*

Rahul's focus is on making sure that everyone has a chance to discuss the issues and practice their communication skills, but, as in real life, the learners' language is not always as good as it could be. The balance between stopping a discussion to give feedback and letting the discussion go on in order to give as much language practice as possible is tricky. Rahul tries hard to only focus on issues which cause miscommunication, perhaps building on comments by the note takers, but this is not always easy in the moment. The one area he always gives feedback on, however, is the written tasks that the case study might require. These are always sent to him by email, and he always sends his feedback before the next lesson. Each lesson has a different focus, depending on the task. He is proud of this achievement, which is a challenge with his busy schedule, but he feels it is important.

Principle 6. *Engage and Collaborate Within a Community of Practice*

Rahul has regular contact with other lecturers in the university, and they often discuss class related issues. He meets frequently with subject specialists to go through the feedback on the case studies, and this often results in edits or even new case studies. He keeps a daily journal to reflect on how the lesson has gone. Sometimes he only writes a few lines, but over the years, the journal has grown into a significant body of work, and he has found it to be a very useful tool in his own development as a teacher. One day he hopes to edit it and perhaps publish it.

Training Sales Engineers to Negotiate in English

Mercedes is employed full time by an automotive company in Mexico. The company makes parts and components for customers all over the world, and Mercedes is a member of the training department with specific responsibility for English language training. She has two main roles.

The first is as a language consultant, which means that anyone in the company can call on her for advice regarding communication in English. The tasks can be quite wide-ranging. Sometimes she is asked to proofread a report or an email, sometimes she is asked to assess the English language skills of people interviewing for a job at the company, and sometimes she is asked to attend meetings as an observer and comment on the effectiveness of employee communication skills. She loves this part of the job, and she never knows what each day will bring.

The second role concerns the training of company employees. She is responsible for making sure that all employees have access to the language training they need in order to do their jobs effectively. A lot of this training is outsourced, and one of her regular tasks is to find local language schools and freelance trainers who can provide suitable instruction. As a trained language teacher, she also runs courses herself, either because suitable providers cannot be found or because the course is so specific that her insider knowledge is critical to its success. At present, her department has been asked to provide a three-day training course for a group of sales engineers who will be travelling to key meetings with clients in order to discuss and negotiate technical specifications and prices, and who want to brush up their English.

Principle 1. *Know Your Learners*

Mercedes looks through the attendance list and realizes that she knows most of the people in the class, although she does not know them well. She does, however, know how to find out more, and she starts by calling their manager to discuss exactly what they need to be able to do. From experience, she knows that these insights will be invaluable, particularly as the manager has been doing the job for several years. He tells her a lot about the situations they will be facing and gives her ideas about possible role plays and simulations that she can use in the course. He also sends her a copy of the company's Global Terms, which have recently been revised, as well as some information about the products the learners will be discussing. She has seen similar documents many times over the years but is not familiar with these since they have been designed for specific customers. She then calls other supervisors and managers in the company who may be able to give her additional information. These include the HR department, which sends her information about courses the sales engineers have attended and an outline of their individual experience as negotiators.

There are eight participants in the course. Six are Mexican and have worked at the company for several years. The other two are new. One is German and one is Chinese. Both are experienced sales engineers, but they are not familiar with the company and its procedures. Mercedes arranges a short telephone call with each learner to discuss the course aims, reasons for the training, and the types of activities she intends to run. She asks about everyone's priorities and expectations. This conversation is in English, which also gives her a chance to informally assess their language proficiency.

Finally, Mercedes arranges a meeting with two of her former learners who are now in other departments. They worked as sales engineers for several years and are also very familiar with the requirements of the job. She discusses the course aims and collects additional ideas for role plays and simulations. She is pleased when they agree to read through and check her initial drafts of role plays and simulations so that they are as close to real-life tasks as possible.

Once Mercedes has collected all this information, she needs to assess the learners' language skills in order to make the three days as efficient as possible. She decides on task-based assessment and, together with her informants, designs a typical task that will give her some idea of the learners' competence. The task involves reading part of a contract (terms of delivery); writing an email to an imaginary client to explain that the agreed delivery terms cannot be met because of problems with tooling (the client's original specifications were incorrect); and seeking to arrange a conference call with the appropriate employees to discuss new delivery dates and a solution to the problem.

As the task is in process in class, Mercedes asks one of her former learners to play the role of the annoyed client in the role play. She listens in to the conference call and makes notes about how well the learners handle the situation. This feeds into her understanding of what the learners can and cannot do. She then checks each email for message content and language use, and considers the following questions for each learner:

	Exceeding Expectations	Meeting Expectations	Approaching Expectations	Not Meeting Expectations
Was the learner able to explain the situation in the email?				
Was the learner able to explain the situation verbally in the conference call?				
Was the learner able to suggest appropriate delays and work towards a solution to the problem?				

Principle 2. *Create Conditions for Language Learning*

The participants know the importance of the course and the need to improve their English, but like most busy people they need to be convinced that the course will be both efficient and effective. Mercedes arranges for their manager to come in during the first hour and speak to them about their upcoming negotiations, as well as give some background information about why and how the course was designed. Mercedes outlines the course content, and the manager explains how he was personally involved in designing some of the activities. Knowing that senior management is interested enough to help design the course activities and follow their progress goes a long way toward increasing the learners' motivation. After the manager leaves, Mercedes emphasizes that she is the language expert, not an experienced sales engineer, and that everyone is free to contribute with task feedback. They are all equal partners in the endeavor, and they all have the same aim.

Principle 3. *Design High-Quality Lessons for Language Development*

Most of the work has been done during the build-up to the course, and there will be little time to adjust things once the course starts. Mercedes is confident that the role plays she has written will give the participants plenty of practice in the areas they need to focus on, and that the key language elements of the course are flexible enough to provide useful input for everyone in the group. The participants will see that the course reflects their own specific context, which gives the course high face validity. Mercedes knows that the course outline she has produced is almost identical to other negotiating courses she has run—the only difference is that some of the language activities and all of the role plays have been planned to reflect the products and services that these learners will be dealing with. Figure 5.2 provides the course outline.

FIGURE 5.2 Course Outline

Aim: To practice the language of negotiation in an international business context.

Time	Activity	Description
Day One		
08:30–09:30	Warm up	"Getting to know you" activity. Discussion of course aims.
09:30–10:15	Feedback/Follow-up discussion	Discussion about the types of language used in negotiations/phases of a negotiation: ✔ Relationship-building ✔ Questions ✔ Exploring interests ✔ Bargaining ✔ Persuasion ✔ Dealing with problems
10:15–10:30	Coffee break	
10:30–12:30	Relationship building	Techniques for relationship building in an intercultural context (e.g., small talk, building rapport, developing trust, impression management)
12:30–13:30	Lunch	

(continued)

FIGURE 5.2	Course Outline *(continued)*	

Day One *(continued)*

13:30–15:15	Questions	Open/closed question techniques Fixed choice questions (grammar focus–question formulation)
15:15–15:30	Coffee break	
15:30–16:30	Exploring interests	Positions vs. interests
16:30–17:00	Feedback and reflection	

Day Two

08:30–09:30	Role play	Warm up
09:30–10:15	Bargaining	Proposing (grammar focus: conditionals)
10:15–10:30	Coffee break	
10:30–12:30	Persuasion Closing the negotiation	Key strategies Summarizing and clarifying Dealing with problems/conflict
12:30–13:30	Lunch	
13:30–16:15	Role play	
16:15–17:00	Feedback and reflection	

Day Three

08:30–09:00	Discussion and lessons learned from previous day	Warm up
09:00–10:15	Vocabulary building	Key vocabulary from company documentation
10:15–10:30	Coffee break	
10:30–12:30	Role play	
12:30–13:30	Lunch	
13:30–16:15	Role play (continued)	
16:15–17:00	Feedback and reflection	

Principle 4. *Adapt Lesson Delivery as Needed*

The activities are designed to be flexible, and Mercedes has more than enough extra activities in her bag should they be required. She soon finds out that the two new members of the group (the German and Chinese sales engineers) bring fresh perspectives to the feedback sessions, and she can draw on their experience to showcase insights the others are not aware of. For example, in the session on small talk, the Mexicans, the Chinese, and the German have very different ideas about the appropriateness of certain topics. Some of the discussions like this, although unplanned, are wide ranging and useful for everyone in the group, and Mercedes is happy to adjust the schedule accordingly.

Principle 5. *Monitor and Assess Learner Language Development*

Mercedes gives regular language feedback throughout the three days, although she is careful never to interrupt a role play while it is going on. She has everyone's permission to video record the role plays and selects short excerpts to use in her feedback sessions. In the final reflection session, she asks the learners to complete a form that will help her evaluate the course. She finishes the course with an end-of-course group discussion, which is attended by the manager. In the final reflection session, Mercedes asks the learners to complete a form that will help her evaluate the course (see figure 5.3).

Principle 6. *Engage and Collaborate Within a Community of Practice*

Mercedes is a member of a group of Mexico-based trainers and HR managers who meet once a year to share ideas and discuss corporate training issues. As one of the few language trainers in the group, she brings her own perspective to the discussions, but she appreciates the chance to network with others in her field. She is also a member of a corporate language trainer's group on social media, and regularly contributes to discussions in the various chat groups. This group is very active and has members from all over the world, and she feels it is a useful contribution to her own continuous professional development. Her company also pays for her to attend one language conference a year, and she normally attends the annual TESOL Convention in the United States whenever she can.

Preparing Indonesian Healthcare Workers for Overseas Employment

Sandra is originally from Louisiana, has a master's degree in TESOL, and now works for a private language school in Indonesia. The school has recently accepted a contract from an agency to prepare Indonesian healthcare workers to work overseas in countries where English is not the first language, but will be used some of the time. Although all the caregivers have already passed

FIGURE 5.3. Reflection form

Take some time to reflect on the course content. Please make notes below:

The most useful activity was:

The least useful activity was:

I did well on:

I need to work more on:

My next step is:

a commercially available English test as part the requirements of their future employees, their agency has realized that these caregivers need more than "general" English and would benefit from more specific training. This has nothing to do with benevolence—several caregivers have been sent home in recent months, which has cost the agency time and money. Agency staff have decided that the general test, while well known and relatively easy to administer, does not test any specific healthcare language skills or knowledge. They have asked the language school to focus on two areas—language for interacting with other healthcare professionals, and language for interacting with patients whose first language is not English. Sandra has been asked to put together a five-day course.

Principle 1. *Know Your Learners*

The first thing Sandra does is make a list of all the possible stakeholders. These include the learners and the agency, but she knows that speaking to former caregivers who have already worked in other countries will be invaluable. She also finds out that a test specifically aimed at healthcare professionals [Occupational English Test (OET)] has recently come on the market. Although passing this test is not a requirement of the course, she realizes that its content will provide useful insights.

Sandra's initial research with the agency tells her that all the caregivers will be working in the Middle East. Some of the work will be with locals, but some will also involve foreign expats, so English skills will be needed. Agency staff explain that although Indonesia is the largest Muslim country in the world, the caregivers will have to be prepared to deal with a different Muslim culture in the Middle East, and that this has not been easy in the past. The agency wants the course to deal with this issue as well as the two language-related aims mentioned above. Sandra feels that this aspect of communication is outside her own experience, and persuades her manager to pay for an experienced caregiver (Dara) to join her in the classroom. Sandra's job will be to focus on language, and Dara will be there to share her professional knowledge as well as her experiences in the Middle East.

Sandra then turns to the learners. She finds that, in addition to having basic English language skills, the learners are all qualified caregivers, having attended courses ranging from six months to two years, as well as a minimum of one year of work experience. They will be applying for jobs in hospitals, hospices, and old age homes in the Middle East. Most, but not all, of the caregivers are female. They do not know each other.

Principle 2. *Create Conditions for Language Learning*

Sandra knows that she does not have a lot of time, so the lessons she gives will need to be meaningful and relevant. She is aware that she will have to build trust with the learners, particularly as she herself has no experience with nursing, but she knows that having Dara in the class will help to allay fears of the unknown and provide valuable professional insights. Luckily, she speaks a little Bahasa Indonesia, and decides to start the class by introducing herself in that language. She knows that her language is full of errors, but her aim is to show that language errors do not prevent communication. Using Bahasa Indonesia will be a bit of fun and help to relax the learners. She also decides to allow time for the learners to get to know each other and builds this into the first morning's program.

Principle 3. *Design High-Quality Lessons for Language Development*

Further study of the OET test, as well as a detailed perusal of commercially available coursebooks on nursing English, have given Sandra very useful ideas for a possible curriculum, and since the agency has given her very specific objectives—language for interacting with other healthcare professionals, and language for interacting with patients whose first language is not English—she decides that the main focus will need to be on speaking and listening skills. She also decides that a task-based approach will be most appropriate. Not only will such an approach allow the caregivers to role play the language they will be using, but she will be able to give timely feedback as necessary. With only five days for the course, there will be no time to think about other language skills such as reading or writing.

Sandra works with Dara to create realistic caregiver–patient role plays, and they agree that the Clinical Communication Criteria (see Table 5.1 below) from the OET Speaking Test will be very useful in evaluating the language and communication strategies used. To practice the language for interacting with other healthcare professionals, Sandra decides that the class will watch the role plays between the caregivers and their "patients" and then discuss the healthcare issues immediately afterwards.

Table 5.1   Clinical Communication Criteria

A. **Indicators of relationship building**
   A1   initiating the interaction appropriately (greetings, introductions, nature of interview)
   A2   demonstrating an attentive and respectful attitude
   A3   adopting a non-judgmental approach
   A4   showing empathy for feelings/predicament/emotional state

B. **Indicators of understanding & incorporating the patient's perspective**
   B1   eliciting and exploring the patient's ideas/concerns/expectations
   B2   picking up the patient's cues
   B3   relating explanations to elicited ideas/concerns/expectations

C. **Indicators of structure**
   C1   sequencing the interview purposefully and logically
   C2   signposting changes in topic
   C3   using organizing techniques in explanations

D. **Indicators for information gathering**
   D1   facilitating the patient's narrative with active listening techniques, minimizing interruption
   D2   using initially open questions, appropriately moving to closed questions
   D3   NOT using compound questions/leading questions
   D4   clarifying statements which are vague or need amplification
   D5   summarizing information to encourage correction/invite further information

E. **Indicators for information giving**
   E1   establishing initially what the patient already knows
   E2   pausing periodically when giving information, using the response to guide next steps
   E3   encouraging the patient to contribute reactions/feelings
   E4   checking whether the patient has understood information
   E5   discovering what further information the patient needs

Source:https://prod-wp-content.occupationalenglishtest.org/resources/uploads/2018/08/22102547/speaking-assessment-criteria-updated-2018.pdf

Principle 4. *Adapt Lesson Delivery as Needed*

Sandra decides to remain very flexible with the activities, but makes sure that she has a sufficient number of role plays to fill the time. She knows that a lot of learning will come through the discussion and feedback after the role plays. Her basic plan is as follows:

1. Divide the group into groups of three. One learner plays the caregiver, the second plays the patient, and the third takes on the role of a health professional watching the interaction. Remaining learners act as language observers to take notes on the communication they thought was good as well as communication they thought could be improved.
2. Each caregiver and each patient receive their role cards and are given time to read and understand the situation. The health professionals and language observers get copies of both roles.
3. The pairs carry out the role plays, while the health professionals and language observers watch and take notes. Sandra and Dara also watch and take notes.
4. Once the role play is over, one health professional pairs up with a health professional from another group and they tell each other what they have just observed. The caregivers and patients listen in.
5. Dara gives feedback from a health professional perspective.
6. Finally, Sandra and the language observers give feedback on the language used.

Sandra never knows exactly how long each cycle will take, but she sees that the learners are enjoying the role playing and that learning and confidence building is taking place. The role plays are varied, and since they test professional knowledge as well as language skills, the follow-up discussions are lively and focused.

Principle 5. *Monitor and Assess Learner Language Development*

Sandra's main tasks in the classroom are to manage the classroom interactions and give language feedback, but she finds that even with the OET criteria she is not always sure if the language and approach used in the role plays is acceptable or appropriate. She relies on Dara's professional knowledge and is happy to do so. As a TESOL professional, she knows that this often happens in ESP classes. Together she feels they make a great team.

Principle 6. *Engage and Collaborate within a Community of Practice*

Sandra learns that the school will probably be running more courses in the future, and she decides that she needs to learn more about teaching English for health professionals. This would not be a one-off course. After some internet research, she finds that there are other teachers in a similar situation, and that they have formed an online group to share ideas and approaches. She joins the group and begins to pose questions. Perhaps one day she will be able to attend an English for Medical Purposes conference in the United Kingdom, but this is not realistic now.

A Look Back and Final Observations

The 6 Principles is a framework for high-quality instruction that can be used in any teaching context. Chapter 5 describes five different ESP classes, but it could easily have included 500, each unique in its own way. Successful ESP classes depend on a thorough needs analysis, and often the teacher is not an expert in the discourse or subject matter which must be addressed. This means that the teacher becomes a partner in the learning process, relying on the knowledge and experience not only of the learners in the class, but potentially a wide range of other stakeholders and resources, which can be exploited to good use. Here are some takeaways to consider:

- ESP classes are unique. Each learner has his or her own needs, which must be considered, as well as the needs of various other stakeholders.
- ESP teachers must know their own limitations. They are rarely the sole experts in the room, and indeed often need to rely on other expert knowledge and input in order to meet the objectives. They must be prepared to ask for help.
- Learning specialized English is not only about what happens in the classroom. ESP teachers spend a lot of time outside the classroom gathering and analyzing the data they need, and then designing and delivering a course that meets the agreed-upon objectives.
- ESP teachers are flexible. They must be prepared to adapt as new information becomes known and if one-off activities do not work quite as well as planned.

Exemplary English language instruction is possible in all contexts where English is taught for a specific purpose—in an academic, workplace, or professional setting—when The 6 Principles are the guide. Instructors use their knowledge of the language skills their learners will need, as well as input from learners themselves and from other professionals in the learners' target fields and disciplines, to connect their instruction directly to learners' goals. They use a range of teaching strategies and techniques so that instruction is relevant to the learners and actively engages them in using English as they will be using it in academic coursework or in their professional work. Teachers monitor and assess the progress their learners are making and provide feedback to advance learners' English skills and give them strategies for continuing to improve their English after the course ends. They engage in communities of practice for their own professional development and to collaborate with others in the field. Other educators and administrators can play a role as well in bringing The 6 Principles to life in the universities, schools, and training programs where English for a variety of specific purposes is taught.

Additional resources for this book are available at www.the6principles.org/eap-esp.

APPENDIX GLOSSARY AND REFERENCES

Appendix

Self-Assessment: The 6 Principles Checklist for Teachers

Do you know your learners? (Principle 1)

___ You gain information about your learners.

    For example, you

    ___ conduct intake protocols and a needs assessment

    ___ organize and share information with other teachers

___ You embrace and leverage the resources your learners bring to the classroom to enhance learning.

    For example, you

    ___ create forms and/or use individual meetings and informal interactions to get to know your learners

    ___ act as a cultural mediator among your learners and between your learners and others in the university or professional context

    ___ draw on learners' native languages and cultures to build rich understandings

Do you create conditions for language learning? (Principle 2)

___ You promote a supportive learning environment, with attention to reducing learners' anxiety and developing trust.

    For example, you

    ___ create a welcoming environment for the learners

    ___ use advance organizers, learning management systems, and syllabuses to provide learning objectives and other information

    ___ design appropriate learning spaces

    ___ identify mentors for new learners

    ___ use clear, patterned, and routine language to communicate with learners

___ You demonstrate expectations of success for all your learners.

    For example, you

    ___ believe all learners will achieve their learning objectives and outcomes

    ___ praise effort and persistence and use critique appropriately

    ___ use a variety of instructional approaches for diverse learners

    ___ teach learners strategies to participate in instructional conversations and in contexts beyond the classroom

___ You plan instruction to enhance and support learners' motivation for language learning.

    For example, you

    ___ prompt learners to connect their learning to their own situations and goals

    ___ build a repertoire of learning tasks that learners enjoy

    ___ motivate learners and structure behavior with well-defined projects

    ___ expect learner ownership and support learners in engagement with learning

Do you design high-quality lessons for language development? (Principle 3)

___ **You prepare lessons with clear outcomes and convey them to your learners.**

For example, you

- ___ develop content and language objectives aligned to learning outcomes
- ___ develop lessons with step-by-step achievement of learning objectives in mind
- ___ communicate learning objectives to learners

___ **You provide and enhance input through varied approaches, techniques, and modalities.**

For example, you

- ___ use comprehensible input to convey information to learners
- ___ adjust your language to enhance input to learners
- ___ use multiple sources of input
- ___ communicate clear instructions for lesson tasks

___ **You engage learners in the use and practice of authentic language and materials.**

For example, you

- ___ elicit output from learners
- ___ create opportunities for learners to be active participants
- ___ use techniques to promote active language practice in a variety of settings
- ___ integrate language learning into content lessons and content into language lessons
- ___ encourage language learning beyond the classroom

___ **You design lessons so learners engage with relevant and meaningful content.**

For example, you

- ___ plan tasks that are relevant and useful
- ___ select materials that reflect learners' interests and goals

___ **You plan differentiated instruction according to your learners' English language proficiency levels, needs, and goals.**

For example, you

- ___ build scaffolding into lessons for different purposes
- ___ employ grouping patterns designed to promote peer support, engagement, and comprehensibility
- ___ provide supplemental materials
- ___ plan for appropriate challenges depending on learners' language proficiency levels

___ **You promote the use of learning strategies, problem-solving skills, and critical thinking.**

For example, you

- ___ teach a variety of learning strategies for specific purposes
- ___ design tasks for learners to practice using critical thinking and learning strategies

___ **You promote self-directed learning.**

For example, you

- ___ facilitate learners' setting of meaningful goals and monitoring of their progress
- ___ provide self-assessment tools that allow learners to evaluate their strengths and weaknesses
- ___ help learners develop effective work management habits

Do you adapt lesson delivery as needed? (Principle 4)

___ You check comprehension frequently and adjust instruction according to learner responses.

For example, you

___ use teaching practices that ensure better auditory comprehension

___ check comprehension with group response techniques

___ You adjust your talk, the task, or the materials according to learner responses.

For example, you

___ adjust your oral language input as needed to advance comprehension and scaffold language learning

___ switch to other forms of input as needed

___ adapt tasks and/or materials to learner proficiency levels

___ scaffold to provide equitable access to content for all learners

Do you monitor and assess learner language development? (Principle 5)

___ You monitor learner errors.

For example, you

___ note errors to provide appropriate feedback to learners

___ reteach when errors indicate learners misunderstood or learned the material incorrectly

___ You provide ongoing feedback effectively and strategically.

For example, you

___ use specific feedback

___ deliver feedback in a timely manner

___ deliver feedback according to the preferences and proficiency level of your learners

___ use a feedforward approach

___ use a variety of types of oral corrective feedback

___ use written feedback when possible

___ You use effective formative and summative assessment strategies.

For example, you

___ use classroom-based assessment to inform teaching and improve learning

___ use testing procedures based on principles of assessment

___ rely on a variety of assessment types.

Do you engage and collaborate within a community of practice? (Principle 6)

___ You are fully engaged in your profession.

For example, you

___ engage in reflective practice

___ participate in continuous learning and ongoing professional development

___ **You coordinate and collaborate with colleagues.**

For example, you

___ meet with colleagues regularly to co-plan for future learning

___ develop and strengthen relationships with program colleagues who can serve as mentors

___ meet with industry and subject matter experts in the professional and occupational fields that your EOP and EPP learners wish to pursue

___ confer with professors or teachers whose courses your EAP learners plan to enter

Glossary

Academic language: A register of the English language; the formal variety of language used for academic purposes (e.g., in academic conversations, lectures, and textbooks) and connected with literacy and academic achievement. Includes reading, writing, listening, and speaking skills used to acquire new knowledge and accomplish academic tasks. In the United States, sometimes known as academic English.

Accommodation (in speaking): The adjusting of language to an interlocutor's speech style in order to aid understanding.

Accommodation (in testing): A change in an assessment itself or the way in which it is administered, intended to make the test results more accurate by creating conditions that allow a test taker to demonstrate his or her knowledge or skills. Examples include allowing extended time and permitting the use of a bilingual glossary.

Authentic language: Language that has not been modified or simplified. Typically refers to language that is produced for a proficient audience and created by a proficient speaker to convey a message.

Authentic practice: Tasks which would be typically performed by proficient speakers of English to expose learners to opportunities to engage with the language and with others. Authentic practice is often done to engage learners in scenarios they will encounter while interacting in English in an English-speaking environment or with very proficient speakers of English.

Benchmark assessment: A short assessment administered at regular intervals to give teachers feedback on how well learners are meeting the academic standards that have been set; a tool to measure learner growth and tailor curriculum or design an intervention to meet individual learning needs. Sometimes known as *formative assessment*.

Bilingual education: A school program using two languages, typically the native language of some learners and a target language. The amount of time and the subject(s) in each language depend on the type of bilingual program, its specific objectives, and learners' level of language proficiency.

The Common European Framework of Reference for Languages (CEFR): A framework developed by Council of Europe "to provide a transparent, coherent and comprehensive basis for the elaboration of language syllabuses and curriculum guidelines, the design of teaching and learning materials, and the assessment of foreign language proficiency." https://www.coe.int/en/web/common-european-framework-reference-languages

Collaborative inquiry: Activity of a group of educators studying together to improve their practice. They identify a problem or critical question, research the topic, and decide what data they need to answer the question. They collect and analyze data, solve the problem/answer the critical question, and share their findings with colleagues. This process may be a cyclical form of teacher professional learning. Also known as *practitioner inquiry* or *action research*.

Collaborative learning: An approach to teaching in which learners spend the majority of class time working in pairs and small groups. They work as team members, talking and discussing, dividing tasks, and taking turns with different roles. Also known as *cooperative learning*.

Collocations: Words or terms that occur together in a language more frequently than chance would predict and that are used as fixed expressions (e.g., fast food, take a break, go online).

Communicative competence: A framework that consists of four areas of competence: linguistic, sociolinguistic, discourse, and strategic.

Communicative task/language analysis (CT/LA): Breaking down the communication tasks identified in a needs assessment into performance objectives based on a communicative competence framework.

Community of practice: A group of people who engage in a process of collective learning as they practice their profession. Each group member brings his or her own skill set, and the group actively shares knowledge, resources, experiences, and orientations to their work, while strengthening their relationships with one another, to enhance their collaborative efforts. Coined by Lave and Wegner (1991).

Comprehensible input: Oral or written input (e.g., new information) to the learner, structured or presented in such a way as to help him or her negotiate the meaning of the communication (e.g., through visuals, gestures, annotations). Over time, the input may increase in the complexity of the language structures used or the amount of information shared.

Criterion references: Measures of a learner's mastery of the material; rather than measuring performance in relation to other learners' scores or grades, criterion-referenced assessments measure individual learners' performance in relation to a standard or learning goal.

Cultural diversity: The variety of cultures that learners bring to an educational setting or may have to deal with in their target situation. Culture includes the customs, lifestyle, traditions, attitudes, norms of behavior, and artifacts of a given group of people. Culturally diverse learners may have different races, ethnicities, languages, professional backgrounds, and socioeconomic status. A goal in the classroom is to respect and honor diverse cultures and build on different ways of knowing or interpreting the world.

Culturally responsive instruction: An approach to classroom instruction that respects and builds on the different cultural characteristics of all learners and ensures that academic discussions are open to different cultural views and perspectives. Learners' ways of knowing are elicited, pedagogical materials are multicultural, and values are shared and affirmed. Also known as culturally responsive teaching or culturally relevant teaching.

Diagnostic tests: Tests that are used pre-instruction to identify learner difficulties and to inform decisions related to curriculum and lesson planning. Diagnostics identify strengths and weaknesses of individuals and the group of learners and often evaluate the four skills of reading, writing, speaking and listening as well as other areas, such as academic skills and strategies.

Discourse: A sequence of utterances—spoken or written sentences—that form a larger unit in a specific social context. Examples include a dinner conversation, a staff meeting, an academic lecture, a weather report.

Discourse analysis: Studying written or spoken language as it is used in real life situations.

Discourse community: A group of people who communicate in a certain way. According to Swales (1990), a discourse community has a broadly agreed set of common public goals, has mechanisms of intercommunication among its members, uses its participatory mechanisms primarily to provide information and feedback, utilizes and hence possesses one or more genres in the communicative furtherance of its aims, has acquired specific lexis, and has a threshold level of members with a suitable degree of relevant content and discoursal expertise.

Dynamic bilingualism: The ability to use more than one language flexibly and strategically, depending on the audience, the conversational partners, or the situation.

English as a foreign language (EFL): The teaching and learning of English in countries where English is not the official language.

English as a lingua franca: Communication in the English language between speakers with different first languages.

English as a medium of instruction (EMI): The use of English by the teacher to teach the subject matter. EMI is increasingly popular in higher education contexts in countries where English is not the dominant language.

English as a second language (ESL): The teaching and learning of English in countries where English is the (or one of the) dominant language. May refer to the language teaching specialists and their teaching certifications or endorsements, or may refer to the learners (i.e., ESL students).

English for academic purposes (EAP): The language and related practices learners require to engage in study or work in English-medium higher education. The focus is to instruct learners on the linguistic, cultural and institutional practices within different academic disciplines.

English for occupational purposes (EOP): The language and related practices learners require to function in English-medium workplaces. Often used synonymously with workplace language training.

English for professional purposes (EPP): The language and related practices learners require to function in English-medium professional contexts, such as business, law, government, or medicine.

English for specific purposes (ESP): EFL/ESL instruction designed around the specific professional, occupational, or academic needs of the learners. An umbrella term that includes EAP, EOP, and EPP.

English language proficiency (ELP) standards: Sets of concise statements identifying the knowledge and skills that English learners are expected to possess in English; statement-by-statement articulations of what learners are expected to learn and what training programs or courses are expected to teach. May refer to national, state, or district standards.

English learners (ELs)/English language learners (ELLs): Children and adults who are learning English as a second, foreign, additional, or new language, at various levels of proficiency. English learners may also be referred to as limited English proficient (LEP), emergent bilinguals (EBs), and nonnative speakers (NNS).

English speakers of other languages (ESOL): Learners whose first language is not English and who do not write, speak, or understand the English language well. In some regions, this term also refers to the programs and classes for English learners.

English-speaking countries: Countries where English is the primary language of the majority of the population, such as the United Kingdom, the United States, Ireland, Canada, Australia, and New Zealand. Because the use of English is widespread in other countries, some qualify those listed above as inner circle English-speaking countries. Note that many smaller nations are also English-speaking countries (e.g., Jamaica, the Bahamas, Trinidad and Tobago, Barbados).

Evaluation: The monitoring of student progress with respect to performance in language development and curricular outcomes using a variety of methods, such as quizzes, tests, exams, portfolios, projects, and presentations.

Feedback: A response by the teacher (or peer) to a learner's output with the intent of helping the learner with language learning. Common feedback types are the clarification request, repetition, recast, reformulation, explicit correction, and elicitation of self-repair/self-correction.

Filler phrase: A meaningless or redundant expression that speakers use to fill in gaps in their speech (e.g., *I mean, like, you know, the thing is that, stuff like that*).

Flipped learning: An instructional method that moves the lecture or presentation of information outside of the classroom and moves the follow-up activities, in which learners apply the information (e.g., as homework) inside of the classroom.

Formative assessment: Typically, classroom-based assessment of learner performance during instruction. Takes place frequently and is ongoing, involving simple but important techniques such as verbal checks for understanding, teacher-created assessments, and other non-standardized procedures. A type of informal assessment that provides teachers with immediate information on how well a learner is progressing.

Funds of knowledge: Knowledge gained through nonacademic means, usually from family and community members in traditional societies. It may include knowledge of the natural world, agriculture, food preparation, crafts, customs, personal histories, legends, and stories.

Genre: A form of communication that has recognized conventions. Examples include a work memo, a research report, a formal invitation, an editorial, a stand-up comedy routine, an academic lecture.

Genre analysis: The linguistic analysis of a communicative event (written or spoken) that is recognized by an established group or community (e.g., a profession or trade) as having a specific purpose and distinguishing features.

High-frequency words: Words that occur most frequently across many different types of texts and transcripts of language. Most are function words, such as articles (*a/an, the*), prepositions (*in, on, at, of*), auxiliaries (*do, be, have, can, may*), pronouns (*that, I, they, it, what, who*), conjunctions (*and, but, so*), conjunctive adverbs (*finally, however*), or quantifiers (*some, much*). They also include common verbs (*go, take, want, make*), nouns (*way, type, thing*), adjectives (*good, nice, great*), and adverbs (*here, now, sometimes, never, well*). For more, see The New General Service List (www.newgeneralservicelist.org).

Higher order thinking: Thinking that requires more than memorization, recall, and the comprehension of ideas from texts or teacher presentation. Higher order thinking involves using ideas actively: applying, analyzing, evaluating, synthesizing, and creating.

Input: Oral or written language provided to the learner.

Instrumental motivation: The motivation to learn a language or skill, or to accomplish some other goal, due to its utility for personal or professional gains. Learners are instrumentally motivated to learn English when they want to pass a standardized language test, obtain a job, or communicate when travelling in an English-medium country.

Intake assessment: A systematic approach to document learners' skills and knowledge before they begin a course of study. It usually involves the collection and analysis of different types of information: answers on forms and questionnaires, interviews, placement tests, transcripts.

Integrative motivation: The motivation to learn a language or skill, or to accomplish some other goal, due to the desire for personal or professional growth or inclusion as a member in a community. Learners have integrative motivated to learn English when they want to become recognized members of an English-speaking social or professional group.

Intensive English language program (IEP): Full-time programs of English that range between 22 and 30 hours of instruction per week in a classroom environment. The learners spend their time in intensive study, thinking, working, and interacting with peers in English. IEP courses develop language proficiency in a short period of time and are popular in English-medium countries. IEP programs may occur in the public or private sector and often lead to more specific ESP training for the workplace or academia.

Intercultural communication: Citizens of different cultures and countries possess specific cultural rules and norms. Intercultural communication explores the notion of understanding one's own frame of reference to interpret meaning in order to enhance communication with interlocutors from different cultural backgrounds.

Just-in-time teaching: A learner-centered strategy in which the teacher applies feedback from learners to determine what skills or information they need to make progress with a project or task and teaches that to them in small bursts. The advantage is that learners are motivated to obtain this knowledge and have immediate application for what they learn.

Language form: Typically refers to aspects of the structure of a language, such as the patterns, rules, and organization of words. Consists of parts of speech, sentence formation, usage, punctuation, and so on, sometimes referred to as the grammar of a language.

Language function: Typically refers to the specific purpose for which language is being used—to define, compare, persuade, evaluate, and so on.

Language input: Oral or written language that is directed to the learner. Differs from language uptake, which is the language that the learner hears, perceives, and processes.

Language modalities: Ways to refer to the four modalities of listening, speaking, reading and writing.

Language proficiency: A learner's degree of competence or performance in using a language for communicative purposes.

Language training specialist: A term used in workplace and professional settings instead of ESL/EFL teacher (see also "trainer").

Language transfer: A process that occurs when a learner applies knowledge of one language to another, often with regard to vocabulary, sentence construction, phonology, and cognitive skills. Positive transfer can take place when linguistic features and learned patterns of a known language (such as cognates, letter-sound correspondences, or ways to find the main idea in a text) are similar to those in the new language and a learner accurately applies them when learning the new language.

Lesson objective: A statement of what learners will be able to do by the end of the lesson. Its purpose is to focus learners' attention on what is important in the lesson. Teachers may have separate content and language objectives for the same lesson. The content objective relates to the content standards or content curriculum topic, and the language objective states what language skill, form, or function learners need to focus on during the lesson.

Lesson objectives (language, content, and learning strategy): Three kinds of objectives that clearly state what learners will know and/or be able to do at the end of a lesson.

Mainstream classes (in EAP): Classes whose subject matter is a specific area of expertise, such as geology or history or business management, rather than English language.

Mediation (as used in the CEFR): According to the CEFR, ". . . mediation combines reception, production and interaction. Also, in many cases, when we use language it is not just to communicate a message, but rather to develop an idea through what is often called 'languaging' (talking the idea through and hence articulating the thoughts) or to facilitate understanding and communication." https://rm.coe.int/cefr-companion-volume-with-new-descriptors-2018/1680787989, p. 33.

Multilingualism: The use of more than one language by an individual or a community of speakers or within a geographical area. A multilingual person speaks more than one language. A multilingual community consists of a group with speakers of more than one language, but some members of the community may speak only one language.

Needs assessment: An inquiry process that documents the current conditions and the desired conditions of stakeholders. The goal is to use the information to identify approaches that can bridge the gap between the current and the desired conditions. Educators use this process to evaluate learners' skills and to analyze the skills they need to succeed with specific tasks.

Negotiated syllabus: A course plan which takes input from both the teacher and the learners into account.

Occupational English Test (OET): An English language test for healthcare professionals. https://www.occupationalenglishtest.org/.

Output: Oral or written language generated by a learner.

Placement tests: Used for internal purposes, placement tests determine the level of English proficiency of the learner to place learners into the appropriate class in multi-level programs. Tests may vary in length and scope. Institutions adopt varying practices for placement testing, including commercial online testing, in-house tests, and commercial standardized language tests.

Practice: The collective name of activities whose goal is to improve the fluency and accuracy of language use with any subskill (e.g., active listening, speaking, reading, writing, grammar, or vocabulary).

Register: A variety of language that is associated with specific social situations and topic areas. Examples include academic language, legal language, the language of mathematics, or the language of sportscasting.

Scaffolding: Classroom support given to assist learners in learning new information and performing related tasks. Often provided by the teacher through demonstration, modeling, verbal prompts (e.g., questioning), feedback, adapted text, graphic organizers, and language frames, among other techniques. Provided to learners over a period of time but gradually modified and then removed in order to transfer more autonomy to the learner, leading to independence.

Social capital: Resources, affordances, or various forms of support that a person can access through social connections.

Social language: A register of the English language that is also referred to as conversational language and is the basic language proficiency associated with fluency and vocabulary in everyday situations. Most English learners acquire social language more rapidly than academic language.

Speech community: A group of people who share the same language and/or dialect.

Stakeholders: Persons or groups interested in and affected by certain decisions or actions.

Strengths-based approach: An attitude in professional practice. Practitioners focus primarily on each individual's abilities, skills, knowledge, and potential contributions over any weaknesses and special needs they may have.

Summative assessment: A formal assessment, such as an end-of-course exam or a state standardized test. Used to measure learner knowledge over an extended period of time, and may be used to measure growth in a subject area from year to year.

Target language: The language that a person is learning or wishes to learn. Also known as *new language*, *additional language*, *second language*, and *foreign language*.

Trainer: A person who focuses on specific skills in order to improve job performance, rather than the broader, more academic approach commonly associated with teaching.

Translanguaging: The strategic choice to mix two or more languages to serve a specific purpose in a communicative situation or to accomplish a task.

Utterance: A unit of language in spoken or written use; utterance is a broader term than sentence in that it includes spoken language as well as partial sentences.

Utterance control: The ability to produce well-formed, grammatically correct, and coherent language deliberately and purposefully when speaking or writing.

Utterance frame: A partially complete spoken or written sentence that a teacher can provide to help learners express ideas—for example, "I think _____ is relevant because _____"; "The reason I agree with _____ is that _____." Also known as a sentence frame or academic language frame.

Acronyms and Abbreviations

CT/LA	Communicative task/language analysis
EAP	English for academic purposes
EFL	English as a foreign language
ELF	English as a lingua franca
EL/ELL	English learner / English language learner
EOP	English for occupational purposes
EPP	English for professional purposes
ESL	English as a second language
ESOL	English speakers of other languages
ESP	English for specific purposes
IEP	Intensive English program

References

FOREWORD

Scharf, R. (2009). *Common sense is NOT common practice*. Englewood, CO: Hugo House Publishers.

PREFACE

Anthony, L. (2015). The changing role and importance of ESP in Asia. *English as a Global Language Education (EaGLE) Journal, 1, 01–21*.

EMI Oxford Research Group. (2019). Introduction to the EMI Oxford Research Network. Retrieved from http://www.emi.network/.

Friedenberg, J., Kennedy, D., Lomperis, A., Martin, W., & Westerfield, K. (2014). *Effective practices in workplace language training*. Alexandria, VA: TESOL International.

Hellman, A., Harris, K., & Wilbur, A. (2019). *The 6 Principles for exemplary teaching of English learners®: Adult education and workforce development*. Alexandria, VA: TESOL International.

Kirkgöz, Y., & Dikilitaş, K. (2018). Recent developments in ESP/EAP/EMI contexts. In Y. Kirkgöz & K. Dikilitaş (Eds.), Key issues in English for specific purposes in higher education. *English Language Education*, vol. 11. Switzerland: Springer International Publishing.

Neeley, T. (2012, May). Global business speaks English. *Harvard Business Review*. Retrieved from https://hbr.org/2012/05/global-business-speaks-english.

TESOL International. (2018). *The 6 Principles for exemplary teaching of English learners®, Grades K–12*. Alexandria, VA: Author.

CHAPTER 1

Basturkmen, H. (2006). *Ideas and options in English for specific purposes*. Mahwah, NJ: Erlbaum.

Bhatia, V. K. (2008). Genre analysis, ESP and professional practice. *English for Specific Purposes 27*, 161–174.

Brown, J. D. (2016). *Introducing needs analysis and English for specific purposes*. New York: Routledge.

Chung, T., & Nation, P. (2003). Technical vocabulary in specialised texts. *Reading in a Foreign Language 15*, 103–116.

Coxhead, A. (2013). Vocabulary and ESP. In B. Paltridge & S. Starfield (Eds.), *The handbook of English for specific purposes* (pp. 115–132). Boston, MA: Wiley-Blackwell.

Douglas, S. R., & Rosvold, M. (2018). Intercultural communicative competence and English for academic purposes: A synthesis review of the scholarly literature. *The Canadian Journal of Applied Linguistics, 21*(1), 23–42. Retrieved from https://journals.lib.unb.ca/index.php/CJAL/article/view/25337/1882518844.

Dudley-Evans, T., & St. John, M. J. (1998). *Developments in English for specific purposes: A multi-disciplinary approach*. Cambridge, UK: Cambridge University Press.

Flowerdew, J. (2011). Reconciling contrasting approaches to genre analysis: The whole can equal more than the sum of the parts. In D. Belcher, A. M. Johns, & B. Paltridge (Eds.), *New directions in English for specific purposes research* (pp. 119–144). Ann Arbor, MI: University of Michigan Press.

Friedenberg, J., Kennedy, D., Lomperis, A., Martin, W., & Westerfield, K. (2014). *Effective practices in workplace language training: Guidelines for providers of workplace English language training services*. Alexandria, VA: TESOL.

Huhta, M., Vogt, K., Johnson, E., Tulkki, H., & Hall, D. R. (2013). *Needs analysis for language course design: A holistic approach to ESP*. Cambridge, UK: Cambridge University Press.

Hutchinson, T., & Waters, A. (1987). *English for specific purposes: A learning-centered approach*. Cambridge, UK: Cambridge University Press.

Hyland, K. (2008). As can be seen: Lexical bundles and disciplinary variation. *English for Specific Purposes 27*, 4–21.

Hyland, K. (2012). *Disciplinary identities*. Cambridge, UK: Cambridge University Press.

Hyland, K., & Shaw, P. (Eds.). (2016). *The Routledge handbook of English for academic purposes*. London, UK: Routledge.

Jenkins, J. (2007). *English as a lingua franca: Attitude and identity*. Oxford, UK: Oxford University Press.

Lave, J., & Wenger, E. (1991). *Situated learning: Legitimate peripheral participation*. Cambridge, UK: Cambridge University Press.

Lesiak-Bielawska, E. D. (2015). English for specific purposes in historical perspective. *English for Specific Purposes World, 46*. Retrieved from http://www.esp-world.info/Articles_46/E_Lesiak-Bielawska%20ESPinHistoricalPerspective.pdf.

REFERENCES FOR CHAPTER 1, *CONTINUED*

Seidlhofer, B. (2011). Understanding English as a lingua franca. Oxford, UK: Oxford University Press.

Swales, J. (1990). *Genre analysis: English in academic and research settings*. Cambridge, UK: Cambridge University Press.

Wenger, E. (1998). *Communities of practice: Learning, meaning and identity*. Cambridge, UK: Cambridge University Press.

CHAPTER 2

American Council for the Teaching of Foreign Languages. (2012). ACTFL Proficiency Guidelines. Alexandria, VA: Author.

Anderson, S. R., & Lightfoot, D. W. (2002). *The language organ: Linguistics as cognitive physiology*. New York, NY: Cambridge University Press.

Anstrom, K., DiCerbo, P., Butler, F., Katz, A., Millet, J., & Rivera, C. (2010). *A review of the literature on American English: Implications for K–12 English language learners*. Arlington, VA: George Washington University Center for Equity and Excellence in Education.

Appleby, Y. (2010). Who are the learners? In N. Hughes & I. Schwab (Eds.), *Teaching adult literacy: Principles and practice* (pp 29–47). Maidenhead, UK: National Research and Development Center and Open University Press.

August, D., & Shanahan, T. (Eds.). (2006). *Developing literacy in second-language learners: Report of the national literacy panel on language-minority children and youth*. Mahwah, NJ: Erlbaum.

Australian Government Department of Education and Training. (2015). *Australian core skills framework*. Canberra, Australia: The Department of Industry, Innovation, Science, Research and Tertiary Education. Retrieved from https://ala.asn.au/australian-core-skills-framework/.

Baker, S., Lesaux, N., Jayanthi, M., Dimino, J., Proctor, C. P., Morris, J., Gersten, R., Haymond, K., Kieffer, M. J., Linan-Thompson, S., & Newman-Gonchar, R. (2014). *Teaching academic content and literacy to English learners in elementary and middle school* (NCEE 2014–4012). Washington, DC: National Center for Education Evaluation and Regional Assistance (NCEE), Institute of Education Sciences, U.S. Department of Education.

Birdsong, D. (2016). Age of second language acquisition: Critical periods and social concerns. In Nicolaidis, E., & Montari, S. (Eds.), *Bilingualism across the lifespan: Factors moderating language proficiency* (pp. 163–182). Berlin, DE: De Gruyter Mouton. Doi:10.1037/14939-010.

Borgwaldt, S. R., & Joyce, T. (2013). Typology of writing systems. In Borgwaldt, S. R., & Joyce, T. (Eds.), *Typology of writing systems* (pp. 1–11). Amsterdam, NL: John Benjamins.

Brown, S., & Larson-Hall, J. (2012). *Second language acquisition myths*. Ann Arbor, MI: University of Michigan Press.

Centre for Canadian Language Benchmarks. (2012). *Canadian Language Benchmarks: English as a second language for adults*. Ottawa, Ontario, Canada: Author. Retrieved from https://www.canada.ca/content/dam/ircc/migration/ircc/english/pdf/pub/language-benchmarks.pdf

Council of Europe. (2018). *Common European framework of reference for languages*. Strasbourg Cedex, France: Council of Europe. Retrieved from https://rm.coe.int/cefr-companion-volume-with-new-descriptors-2018/1680787989.

De Angelis, G. (2007). *Third or additional language acquisition*. Clevedon, UK: Multilingual Matters.

DeKeyser, R. (2010). Practice for second language learning: Don't throw out the baby with the bathwater. *International Journal of English Studies, 10*, 155–165.

DeKeyser, R. M. (Ed.). (2007). *Practice in a second language: Perspectives from applied linguistics and cognitive psychology*. New York, NY: Cambridge University Press.

Dörnyei, Z. (2014). Motivation in second language learning. In M. Celce-Murcia, D. M. Brinton, & M. A. Snow (Eds.), *Teaching English as a second or foreign language* (4th ed., pp. 518–531). Boston, MA: National Geographic/Cengage Learning.

Dörnyei, Z., & Ushioda, E. (2011). *Teaching and researching motivation* (2nd ed.). New York, NY: Routledge.

Douglas Fir Group. (2016). A transdisciplinary framework for SLA in a multilingual world. *Modern Language Journal, 100*, S1, 19–47.

Ellis, R. (2017). Oral corrective feedback in L2 classrooms. In H. Nassaji & E. Kartchava (Eds.), *Corrective feedback in second language teaching and learning: Research, theory, applications, implications*. New York, NY: Routledge.

Ellis, R., & Shintani, N. (2014). *Exploring language pedagogy through second language acquisition research*. New York, NY: Routledge.

García, O., Johnson, S. I., & Seltzer, K. (2017). *The translanguaging classroom: Leveraging student bilingualism for learning*. Philadelphia, PA: Caslon.

Gardner, R. C. (1985). *Social psychology and second language learning: The role of attitudes and motivation*. London, UK: Edward Arnold.

Gonzalez, N. E., Moll, L., & Amanti, C. (Eds.). (2005). *Funds of knowledge: Theorizing practices in households, communities, and classrooms*. Mahwah, NJ: Erlbaum.

Grabe, W. (2009). *Reading in a second language: Moving from theory to practice*. New York, NY: Cambridge University Press.

Hafiz, F., & Tudor, I. (1989). Extensive reading and the development of reading skills. *English Language Teaching Journal 43* (1), 4–11.

Hoover, J. J., Baca, L. M., & Klinger, J. K. (Eds.) (2016). *Why do English learners struggle with reading? Distinguishing language acquisition from learning disabilities* (2nd ed.). Thousand Oaks, CA: Corwin.

Knowles, M. S., Holton, E. F. III, & Swanson, R. A. (2015). *The adult learner* (8th ed.). New York, NY: Routledge.

Krashen, S. (1985). *The input hypothesis: Issues and implications*. New York, NY: Longman.

Krekeler, C. (2006). Language for special academic purposes (LSAP) testing: The effect of background knowledge revisited. *Language Testing, 23* (1), 99–130. doi: 10.1191/0265532206lt323oa

Lynch, E. W. (2011). Developing cross-cultural competence. In E. W. Lynch & M. J. Hanson M. J. (Eds.), *Developing cross-cultural competence: A guide for working with children and their families* (4th ed., pp 41–78). Baltimore, MD: Brookes Publishing.

Lyster, R., & Saito, K. (2010). Oral feedback in classroom SLA. *Studies in Second Language Acquisition, 32*, 265–302. Doi: 10.1017/S0272263109990520.

Macalister, J. (2008). Implementing extensive reading in an EAP programme. *English Language Teaching Journal, 62* (3), 248–256. Retrieved from https://doi-org.lib-ezproxy.concordia.ca/10.1093/elt/ccm021.

Mackey, A., Abbuhl, R., & Gass, S. M. (2012). Interactionist approach. In S. Gass & A. Mackey (Eds.), *The Routledge handbook of second language acquisition* (pp. 7–23). New York, NY: Routledge.

Merriam, S. B., & Bierema, L. L. (2014). *Adult learning: Linking theory and practice*. San Francisco, CA: Jossey-Bass.

Muñoz, C. (2011). Input and long-term effects of starting age in foreign language learning. *International Review of Applied Linguistics in Language Teaching, 49* (2), 113–133.

Nagy, W. E., & Scott, J. A. (2000). Vocabulary processes. In M. Kamil, P. Mosenthal, P. D. Pearson, & R. Barr (Eds.), *Handbook of reading research, Volume III* (pp. 269–284). Mahwah, NJ: Erlbaum.

Nassaji, H., & Kartchava, E. (Eds.). (2017). *Corrective feedback in second language teaching and learning: Research, theory, applications, implications*. New York, NY: Routledge.

Nation, I. S. P., & Webb, S. (2011). *Researching and analyzing vocabulary*. Boston, MA: Heinle.

National Academies of Sciences, Engineering, and Medicine (NASEM). (2017). *Promoting the educational success of children and youth learning English: Promising futures*. Washington, DC: The National Academies Press. doi.org/10.17226/24677.

National Research Council. (2012). *Improving adult literacy instruction: Options for practice and research*. Washington, DC: The National Academies Press.

Norton, B. (2013). *Identity and language learning*. Bristol, UK: Multilingual Matters.

Ó Laoire, M., & Singleton, D. (2009). The role of prior knowledge in L3 learning and use: Further evidence of psychotypological dimensions. In B. Hufeisen & L. Aronin (Eds.), *The exploration of multilingualism: Development of research on L3, multilingualism, and multiple language acquisition* (pp. 79–102). Amsterdam, Netherlands: John Benjamins.

Parrish, B., & Johnson, K. (2010). *Promoting learner transitions to postsecondary education and work: Developing academic readiness skills from the beginning*. CAELA Network Briefs. Washington, DC: Center for Applied Linguistics.

Patterson, M. B. (2018). The forgotten 90%: Adult nonparticipation in education. *Adult Education Quarterly, 68* (1), 41–62. https://doi.org/10.1177/0741713617731810.

REFERENCES FOR CHAPTER 2, *CONTINUED*

Pavlenko, A., & Norton, B. (2007). Imagined communities, identity, and English language teaching. In J. Cummins & C. Davidson (Eds.), *International handbook of English language teaching* (pp. 669–680). New York, NY: Springer.

Pearson English. (n.d.). Global Scale of English. Retrieved from https://www.pearson.com/english/en/about/gse.html.

Rex, L. A., & Green, J. L. (2008). Classroom discourse and interaction: Reading across the traditions. In B. Spolsky & F. M. Hult (Eds.), *The handbook of educational linguistics* (pp. 571–584). Malden, MA: Blackwell.

Rutgers, D., & Evans, M. (2015). Bilingual education and L3 learning: Metalinguistic advantage or not? *International Journal of Bilingual Education and Bilingualism, 20* (7), 788–806. http://dx.doi.org/10.1080/13670050.2015.1103698.

Sandrock, P. (2010). *The keys to assessing language performance*. Alexandria, VA: ACTFL.

Sato, M., & Ballinger, S. (2016). Understanding peer interaction: Research synthesis and directions. In M. Sato & S. Ballinger (Eds.), *Peer interaction and second language learning: Pedagogical potential and research agenda* (pp 1–30). Amsterdam, Netherlands: John Benjamins. doi:10.1075/lllt.45.01int.

Saunders, W. M., & O'Brien, G. (2006). Oral language. In F. Genesee, K. Lindholm-Leary, W. M. Saunders, & D. Christian (Eds.), *Educating English language learners* (pp. 14–63). New York, NY: Cambridge University Press.

Schmitt, N., Jiang, X., & Grabe, W. (2011). The percentage of words known in a text and reading comprehension. *Modern Language Journal, 95*, 6–43.

Short, D., & Echevarría, J. (2016). *Developing academic language with the SIOP Model*. Boston, MA: Pearson.

Swain, M., & Suzuki, W. (2008). Interaction, output, and communicative language learning. In B. Spolsky & F. M. Hult (Eds.), *The handbook of educational linguistics* (pp. 557–570). Malden, MA: Blackwell.

TESOL International. (2018). *The 6 Principles for exemplary teaching of English learners, Grades K–12*. Alexandria, VA: Author.

Weingarten, R. (2013). Comparative graphematics. In S. R. Borgwaldt & T. Joyce (Eds.), *Typology of writing systems* (pp. 13–39). Amsterdam, NL: John Benjamins.

Ushioda, E. (2009). A person-in-context relational view of emergent motivation, self and identity. In Z. Dornyei & E. Ushioda (Eds.), *Motivation, language identity and the L2 self* (pp. 215–228). Bristol, UK: Multilingual Matters.

WIDA. (2012). *2012 amplification for the English language development standards, Kindergarten–grade 12*. Madison, WI: Author.

Williams, M., Mercer, S., & Ryan, S. (2015). *Exploring psychology in language learning and teaching*. New York, NY: Oxford University Press.

Zhou, M., & Kim, S. (2006). Community forces, social capital, and educational achievement: The case of supplementary education in the Chinese and Korean immigrant communities. *Harvard Educational Review 76* (1), 1–29. https://doi.org/10.17763/haer.76.1.u08t548554882477.

Zwiers, J. (2014). *Building academic language: Grades 5–12* (2nd ed.). San Francisco, CA: Jossey Bass.

CHAPTER 3

Anderson, L. W., & Krathwohl, D. R. (Eds.). (2001). *Taxonomy for learning, teaching, and assessing: A revision of Bloom's Taxonomy of Educational Objectives*. Boston, MA: Longman.

Bloom, B. S., Engelhart, M. D., Furst, E. J., Hill, W. H., & Krathwohl, D. R. (1956). *Taxonomy of educational objectives: The classification of educational goals. Handbook 1: Cognitive domain*. New York: David McKay Company.

Brinks Lockwood, R. (2014). *Flip it! Strategies for the ESL classroom*. Ann Arbor, MI: University of Michigan Press.

Brinks Lockwood, R. (2018). *Flipping the classroom: What every ESL teacher needs to know*. Ann Arbor, MI: University of Michigan Press.

Buck Institute for Education. (2018). What is project based learning? Retrieved from http://www.bie.org/about/what_pbl.

Chamot, A. U. (2009). *The CALLA handbook: Implementing the cognitive academic language learning approach* (2nd ed.). Boston, MA: Pearson.

Chan, C. S. C., & Frendo, E. (2014). *New ways in teaching business English*. Alexandria, VA: TESOL.

Dewey, J. (1933). *How we think: A restatement of the relation of reflective thinking to the educative process*. Boston, MA: D. C. Heath.

Doran, G. T. (1981). There's a S.M.A.R.T. way to write management's goals and objectives. *Management Review 70* (11), 35–36.

Dweck, C. S. (2006). *Mindset: The new psychology of success*. New York, NY: Random House.

Folse, K. (2004). *Vocabulary myths: Applying second language research to classroom teaching*. Ann Arbor, MI: University of Michigan Press.

Gay, G. (2010). *Culturally responsive teaching and practice* (2nd ed.). Portsmouth, NH: Heinemann.

Harding, K. (2007). *English for specific purposes*. Oxford, UK: Oxford University Press.

Hyland, K. (2004). *Disciplinary discourses: Social interactions in academic writing*. Ann Arbor, MI: University of Michigan Press.

Larrivee, B. (2000). Transforming teaching practice: Becoming the critical reflective teacher. *Reflective Practice 1* (3), 293–297.

Lave, J., & Wenger, E. (1991). *Situated learning: Legitimate peripheral participation*. Cambridge, UK: Cambridge University Press.

Levine, L. N., & McCloskey, M. (2013). *Teaching English language and content in mainstream classes: One class, many paths* (2nd ed.). Boston, MA: Pearson.

Lyster, R., & Saito, K. (2010). Interactional feedback as instructional input. *Language, Interaction, and Acquisition 1* (2), 276–297.

Master, P., & Brinton, D. M. (1997). *New ways in English for specific purposes*. Alexandria, VA: TESOL.

Michaels, S., O'Connor, M. C., Williams Hall, M., & Resnick, L. B. (2013). *Accountable talk sourcebook: For classroom conversation that works*. Retrieved from http://iflpartner.pitt.edu/index.php/educator_resources/accountable_talk.

Nation, I. S. P., & Macalister, J. (2010). *Language curriculum design*. New York, NY: Routledge.

Nieto, S., & Bode, P. (2011). *Affirming diversity: The sociopolitical context of multicultural education* (6th ed.). Boston, MA: Pearson.

Schon, D. A. (1990). *The reflective turn: Case studies in and on educational practice*. New York, NY: Teachers College Press.

Short, D., & Echevarría, J. (2016). *Developing academic language with the SIOP Model*. Boston, MA: Pearson Allyn & Bacon.

Tomlinson, C. A. (2014). *The differentiated classroom: Responding to the needs of all learners* (2nd ed.). Alexandria, VA: Association for Supervision and Curriculum Development.

Zimmerman, B. J., & Schunk, D. H. (2012). An essential dimension of self-regulated learning. In D. H. Schunk & B. J. Zimmerman (Eds.), *Motivation and self-regulated learning: Theory, research, and applications* (pp. 1–30). New York, NY: Routledge.

CHAPTER 4

Banton, J. (2018, June 28). Personal interview.

Blok, S. (2016, May 2). ELT best practice: Intensive English programs in the USA [Blog post]. Retrieved from http://blog.tesol.org/elt-best-practices-intensive-english-programs-in-the-usa/.

Cooper, A. (2017). Administrators in action: Four steps for strengthening your EL program. Retrieved from http://www.colorincolorado.org/blog/administrators-action-four-steps-strengthening-your-el-program.

DePetro Orlando, R. (2016). *Perspectives on teaching English in U.S. university intensive English programs*. Alexandria, VA: TESOL.

Harper, C. A., & de Jong, E. J. (2009). English language teacher expertise: The elephant in the room. *Language & Education: An International Journal 23* (2), 137–151. https://0-doi-org.mercury.concordia.ca/10.1080/09500780802152788.

Heng, T. T. (2017). Voices of Chinese international students in USA colleges: 'I want to tell them that . . . '. *Studies in Higher Education 42* (5), 833–850. doi:10.1080/03075079.2017.1293873.

Lacroix, J. (2018, September 20). The 6 Principles Book Club [Blog post]. Retrieved from http://blog.tesol.org/the-6-principles-book-club/.

Lave, J., & Wenger, E. (1991). *Situated learning: Legitimate peripheral participation*. Cambridge, UK: Cambridge University Press.

Leask, B. (2015). *Internationalising the curriculum*. Abingdon, UK: Routledge.

Leask, B., & Carroll, J. (2011). Moving beyond 'wishing and hoping': internationalisation and student experiences of inclusion and engagement. *Higher Education Research and Development 30* (5), 647–659.

Lin, J.-C. G., & Yi, J. K. (1997). Asian international students' adjustment: Issues and program suggestions. *College Student Journal 31*, 473–479.

REFERENCES FOR CHAPTER 4, *CONTINUED*

Movit, M., Petrykowska, I., & Woodruff, D. (2010). *Using school leadership teams to meet the needs of English language learners*. Information Brief. Washington, DC: National Center on Response to Intervention. Retrieved from http://ea.niusileadscape.org/docs/FINAL_PRODUCTS/LearningCarousel Using_School_Leadership_Teams.pdf.

TESOL. (2008). *Standards for ESL/EFL teachers of adults*. Alexandria, VA: Author.

Theoharis, G., & O'Toole, J. (2011). Leading inclusive ELL: Social justice leadership for English language learners. *Educational Administration Quarterly 47* (4), 646–688.

Volet, S. E., & Ang, G. (1998). Culturally mixed groups on international campuses: An opportunity forInter-cultural learning. *Higher Education Research and Development 17*, 5–23. doi.org/10.1080, 0729436980170101.

www.ingramcontent.com/pod-product-compliance
Ingram Content Group UK Ltd.
Pitfield, Milton Keynes, MK11 3LW, UK
UKHW051259180426
11947UKWH00020B/1801